JOY GOSWAMI

Selected Poems

T0317242

ARTISTS AND WRITERS SERIES

JOY GOSWAMI
Selected Poems

translated from the Bengali

Whale & Star Press

CONTENTS

CONTENTS

CONTENTS

Joy Goswami
A Brief Biography

Joy Goswami was born in Kolkata on November 10, 1954. The family moved to Ranaghat, about 60 km away from Kolkata, sometime after, and it is there he spent most of his formative years. Joy studied up to "XIth standard" before dropping out of the conventional exam-based educational system. He lost his father, an old time Congress party worker and freedom fighter, at a very early age of 8. His mother, who was the Principal of a high school, did a masters in English literature and inculcated the habit of book reading in her son. Joy grew up with his younger brother, among lots of books to read, lots of music albums to listen to, and subject to phases of depression. As a child, he was very introverted. Alone, stray thoughts would come to his mind; sometimes he would write them down. One day, his brother chanced upon his notebook and read out his poems to his friends. Shocked and embarrassed, Joy decided to write in a style that his brother and friends wouldn't understand. The process – of both trying to give vent to his thoughts, as well as to hide what he was trying to express – became a stylistic feature of Joy's early poems. From 1988 his poetry became more direct, simpler.

The two brothers did not know what to do and how to earn their living after their mother's death in 1984. It was not easy to be a poet, and just a poet, even in a land as respectful of poets as Bengal. Since 1976 Joy had been writing in numerous little magazines and for *"Desh Patrika,"* one of the leading literary magazines published in Kolkata, and finally joined *Desh* to take care of the poetry section. After 30 years in Ranaghat, Joy came back to Kolkata in 1992 and has lived there since. Joy married Kaberi in 1994. He says that living with Kaberi and his daughter Bukun has helped him understand a woman's psyche.

Joy, a great lover of Indian classical music, believes music begins from the point where the words end. But music needn't always have a tune. Any experience that uplifts like music is music for Joy.

Bouts of typhoid and an attack of hepatitis B forced Joy to lead a marginal life. Joy has missed out a lot owing to illness, but that has also sharpened his perspective on life. In a 2002 interview he said – "Even though I write, I feel I'm miserably unsuccessful. Will my poems be able to change the world ravaged by the Gujarat riots? ….. I know my reaction wouldn't help anybody be less cruel. My poems, provide a solace to the bruises of my readers. They can only console, but not cure." Solace, and marvel at the sharp wonder of life, not pessimism, are the hallmarks of Joy's poetry.

Joy's first poems were first published when he was 19. Many followed, often in relatively unknown magazines. His first book of poems came out in 1977, *Christmas o Sheeter Sonet guchchha* (Christmas and a bunch of winter sonnets). The publication cost was borne by his mother. Next, came *Pratnajib* (Ancient life) and *Aleya Hrad* (The lake of the moving lights), back to back. Joy shared a special relationship with his mother and was very dependent on her. When she passed away, Joy, realizing that he was alone in the world, wrote one of his most important collections of poems *Unmader Pathakram*, and immediately after that *Bhutum Bhagaban*. In those poems flashes of the disturbing seventies – the Naxalbari movement, an ultra-left upsurge in West Bengal – also appear.

Today Joy Goswami is one of the most powerful poets of India, one of the best in the post-Jibanananda era of Bengali poetry. Mainly a poet, Joy has also written novels and literary prose. He has more than 30 published books of poems, including three volumes of collected verse, amounting to nearly 1000 poems, long and short. He has also written 12 novels, two in verse, and 5 collections of essays related to interpretation and appreciation of poetry written in Bengali. Goswami has received the most prestigious literary awards of his region and country, the "Ananda purashkaar" prize, twice – in 1990 for *Ghumiyechho Jhaupata?* and in 1998 for *Jara Brishtite Bhijechhilo*. In 1997 he won the Bangla Academy "Puroshkar" award for *Bajrobidyut-bharti Khata* and in the same year also the "Birendra Chattopadhyay Smriti" award for *Patar Poshak*. The Sahitya Academy Award from India's National Academy of Letters came in 2000 for his collection of poems *Paagli Tomar Shangey* (With You, Mad Woman). He also took part in the International Writers workshop at the Iowa State University in 2001.

A very different turn has been taken recently by Joy, in his book of poems *Shashoker Proti* (Addressing the Ruler). By this time, in 2007 he had left *Desh* and joined a newspaper, *Sanbad Protidin*. Meanwhile in Nandigram, West Bengal, at least 14 villagers, protesting against agricultural land acquisition to build a chemical hub, were killed when police opened fire on March 14, 2007. The casualties, West Bengal's worst in 30 years of Left Front rule, sparked off nation-wide protests. Joy took active part in this movement; his poems were used in protest festoons and posters.

The depth of his feeling may be seen in an interview with Sumit Chakrabarti. Joy says – "When there's a mass homicide I also feel the way you feel. This is an expression of a personal grievance which has coalesced with the grievance of the common people. It's not as if I've written these poems as an intellectual…nothing of that sort. I would have written poems of despair if I were sick. Likewise, this despair is on seeing a malady within the society…this angry outburst. I never thought that I would have to speak in public meetings or press conferences against the government. But what happened in Nandigram, the heinous crime that was committed made me decide that I would speak up on this issue. It was a call from within…and so I did it."

Reflections on the Poems of Joy Goswami

Roald Hoffmann

Poetry faces the world in ways that are both internal (to a language and a culture), and external. It was not always so – poetry was once read (actually, recited) only in the language it was written in; even as it touched people's hearts, what foreigners thought was irrelevant. But empires – be they Chinese, Arab or European – and easy conduits of communication both changed that. Conquest, with the attendant imposition of political rule, implied translation; the Hebrew and Christian poets of Al Andalus and its neighboring regions learned, to their benefit, what a ghazal and a divan were. One wanted to co-opt the barbarians – the Chinese were so good at that.

In more benevolent times (some would say, in times of cultural imperialism) translations became available, and, in time, de rigueur for the aspiring intellectual. The elite youth of Renaissance Europe knew their Ovid in the original, but were ignorant of the Bhagavad-gita. Now many more can benefit from both, even if it is only in the partial appreciation that derives from even a sensitive translation.

Within a culture, the universe of poetry was moved by other factors. Great poets always mattered. Perceived and attributed excellence, a kind of capturing of the Zeitgeist that only a poet could perform, was sought out. By rulers to grace their courts, by ordinary people for any simple occasion with emotional import. There was one for every age: Goethe, and not Kleist, was the model German poets emulated, even as they rebelled against the singular Romantic master.

There also evolved, within each language, an accepted way of expression of emotion in a poem. With room for difference, to be sure. But a way that in time differed in small and eventually large ways from expression in other cultures, other languages.

This is a preface to facing straight-on the twin "problems," external and internal, of Bengali poetry in the 21st century – the greatness of Rabindranath Tagore, and what is externally perceived as an accepted mode of sentimentality.

Do I deal in stereotypes? I do. But they must be banished by allowing them to emerge from the dark of our mind.

And will I let Joy Goswami's poetry speak for itself? I will, I will, and his poems do. But let me first address the two problems, real or not.

One might think that in a culture in which the essential spiritual importance of poetry is as manifest as in Bengal – that in such a hospitable clime for the poetic mode there might be many mansions. But in a contemporary *adda*, that unique Bengali gathering for conversation, music, poetry, and a snack – be it set in the wilds of New Jersey or a couple of kilometers away from the hellish approaches to Howrah Bridge – you will be hard-pressed to miss Tagore's presence. Ill-served by fawning, pseudo-spiritual translators, canonized by the Nobel Prize, the sage of Santiniketan also dominates (only in part due to our ignorance) the external image of Bengali poetry. Well-deserved, dear Tagore. Never mind your translators. And… every Bengali poet is defined against you.

As for sentimentality, pathos (well, humor too) is the thing human beings will most differ on. What is profound sentiment to one, is maudlin to another. Yet a language and a time define a mode of expression; and they evolve, dare I say change, at different rates in different poetic cultures. The dance of the primal quartet – self, nature, love, death – has always been the poet's realm. There have been times when the language that sets the dancers in motion was veiled and ornate. Perhaps they will come again, just as postmodern architecture replaced Bauhaus boxes.......

In recent times, in English, the poetic language of choice is frontal and direct. Poets find ways to be different even within accepted conventions; nevertheless, there often is a dominant tone. Indian poetry has long favored allusion and indirection. This was the way to express ineffable longing, the chanced glance across a lawn of a summer afternoon. And sentimentality (and I mean that word positively) in Bengali poetry posed and poses a problem – more for the resultant (in)ability to touch the outsider emotionally in translation, than for the sensitive reader in the original language.

As I write this, I stop myself. For the attribution of "sentimentality" to an act or its description just begs to be deconstructed. Especially when it is applied by a "critic" (often an intellectual) – even more so when he is an outsider, as I am – in a society where so many people are marginalized, economically and in having their simple dignity taken away. Debashis Mukherjee reminded me of this and of the spiritual tie here between the great Bengali filmmaker Ritwik Ghatak and Joy Goswami. In one of Ghatak's films, *Subarnarekha*, a young girl, Sita, takes her life – it is the only thing she can do. In one of Joy's poems, two children steal their mother's corpse and carry it off. Given the context, the actions are <u>appropriate</u>, even as they might seem excessive. Mukherjee asks, "Is portraying these human beings' acts morbid, is reminiscing about them to be considered maudlin, is displaying the intensity of feeling by the individual (or by the writer as he or she allows us to experience that intensity) to be called sentimental?"

The problem ultimately is that of translation, that impossible yet absolutely necessary mapping of language and culture. I am led here to think of the problems of Greek tragedy in our times. How difficult it is to capture in 21st century English the spirit of the chorus of women possessed in Dionysian rites in Euripides' *The Bacchae*!

But I want to write of Joy Goswami's poetry, not the prejudices the reader brings to it. His poems are fierce – in their expression, in the impact of their juxtaposed images, in the effect the images have one on another. The poems possess an immediacy, in our being drawn in pell-mell into the essential tension of real poetry – that just this feeling, just this moment is felt by the writer. That what the words describe is a transformative, searing moment for Goswami. Which is simultaneously and freely a gift to us.

That immediacy of a Goswami poem is to me actually a line stretching to Rabindranath Tagore, in as much as Tagore's work reaches me through his best translators.

There is little sentimentality in Goswami. Curiously, the melancholy and mood-setting does find a place in his novels; in the poems, the place and a person's mood are evoked in breathtaking turns of language. There are dreams, as in "The Lake of Moving Light," but they are jagged dreams. I marvel at what Goswami does in a love poem, as in "This One Noon." Here is the setting to circle gently round the sensual. But Goswami manages something else, the transformation of a real gesture – just this one. Out of the precise determination of a lover's touch, a universe takes shape between two people.

I would say the only giving in to the sentimental, in the broadest sense of the word, might be a reasonably consistent invocation by Goswami of the figure of the poet, as suffering, feeling, overcoming. But then I haven't known a culture where poets are seen otherwise.

Indian society, God knows, leaves plenty to condemn, plenty to mourn, plenty to just get angry with. The older hammer and sickle crowd wanted poets to write the banners, figuratively speaking, that would get others incensed at the injustice all around. A good poem, like Goswami's "Tale of a Funeral," instead finds new ways to take the social and make it personal. The horror is in the person, and in what one human being does to another; the forces that made for that horror may in this way be felt.

Goswami's poems delight in the magic of metamorphoses. And he does it so easily! So in one section of "Garment of Leaf" the protagonist lays down in a field, and

The instant sleep came the field on that side
Put out its hand. Trapped finger between finger.
Pulled me. I
Rose up on tiptoe walked over to that field,
Falling on it, kissing it again and again
Descended into some strange grave.
When the spell broke, there was earth on my back,
Mounds of earth…

The poet touches the field, is integrated into it. And we, we don't blink an eyelid, so easy and natural it is.

Or, if not the poet, then Death (in one section of "Sujyopora Chhai"):

Why he comes and sits on the window
An earthen cup in his hand. As he sips
Down his transparent throat descend
Molten nebulae, a flattened sun, droplets of moon

As above, abstractions and concepts become human actors in Goswami's poem. So in "Victorious,"

Extinction points toward a mountain.

and in "An Essay Concerning Light,"

Piercing the surface rising upwards from the
                    earth's center it began
My autobiography
Cracking layer after layer of rock with its head.

These person/concepts immediately enter a narrative, better said shape a narrative themselves, so that two lines on they are speaking to you as naturally as any character in an evolving story. Quite incredible!

Still another characteristic bit of enchantment Goswami pulls off effortlessly is the imagined conversation, of a woman and a river, or a poet and the muse of his youth ("For a Cloudgirl"):

I was supposed to write,' I said,
'Me it was you asked to write.'

Oh, is it here?' she said to me,
'Throw it in the village pond,
and look,
I'm no more a cloud, you know,
now they call me rain.'

How easy it feels!

The prime feature of the verses of this brilliant Bengali poet is its abundant, leaping imagery. How I hope we capture this in English – the daring that makes a Bengali audience hold its breath as Joy's images dance in its ears, as the mind races to see a breast withering "with the pungent lime," as we stand in paper boats waving hands, as a hornet chases a life, and a dust cloud chases the hornet!

Devasting imagery of war, cruelty and calamity is a recurring feature of Goswami's poems; what astounds is the killing freshness of words, and how it flows in and out of the ordinary world. There is also in his poems a self-deprecating, honest wit – whether Goswami is talking of "glum-faced and always-smiling poets" who emerge uniformed from under the ground. Or, in "Part Autobiography," of a stick put to writing poetry, messing it up, stick-like, reprimanded, and eventually doing it as well as the poet. Maybe the stick is the poet.

One could just float on Goswami's criss-crossing images, savor them on second reading, and hear his crisp and penetrant words. But then one is brought up by meaning – for Joy's words are not just words but make sense. We know, for that is his métier, that their meaning cuts the poet. And cuts through to the center of our emotional universe. Joy Goswami's world is fiercely private. But he does not keep us out, this wonderful poet.

Poems

HAWK OF IRON, FOR YOU

You won't break my trance, hawk of iron, no matter
if you bore a hole in my skull you thrust your beak in
set your two feet on my two shoulders, your taloned
feet, no, my dream won't break hawk of iron, my
eyes are no longer in your grip, yes, my fingers my bones
       my backbone are in your grip, my
getting up and sitting down, blowing my nose,
       my hiccups are in your grip
My bolster, my pillow, my water jug and glass,
my clothes, my doors and windows, my fanfares,
       my music-stand are in your grip, but
my mind has gone from atom
       to elementary particle, it
has taken on the speed of light what can you do to it
       hawk of iron, no matter how much,
boring a hole in my skull you put your beak in
       you'll find no fluid in the brain
          Solid, black, hot,
your beak will fail, twisted, dented, hawk
            of iron, in your
innards a thousand machines clang clank, a
       thousand televisions jingle jangle,
a thousand aeroplanes shriek swooping up and down,
       in collision, spewing blood-money,
handshakes, killing and spy-running but what
can your pepper-and-salt spies, your boy-faced
       spies do to me hawk of iron?
Before me now in a sea of fire climbs
       a fog of firedrops, the sun
floats by, the sun drops, a dead star, and
through a gap in this ocean
of countless suns, I slip out, I reveal myself
       through its other mouth
where before me is a colossal heart with all
its pulsations,
       my eye, a vehicle
lands in it...sends signals, sends signals.
          Ah, distant

most distant signals
prebirth signals
envelop me…

Meanwhile, hawk of iron, you can do as you wish
with this body of mine, I don't care anymore!

Translated by Probir Ghosh

THIS ONE NOON

This one noon I do not sleep, I do not wake, I do not die, I do not live
time enters the room through the window, until this noon I did not
    know my hand,
my own thin hand is a lyre
You grab my hand like a musician seizing his instrument from elbow to
    index finger
and you look at it as if
'what a wonderful thing it is.'
Your lips fall from the tip of my finger, on flash major and minor chords,
    on and on
in my palm you discover a red vein, what a surprise, it trembles,
until this noon I did not know

I knew nothing about water, land, and sky before this noon
I do not sleep, I do not wake, I do not die, I do not live, only a bird
comes and lands on my face
A village falls like a stone into the river and the river changes course
Since that time there is a stream of hill water in place of my home,
I do not drown, I do not float, I do not fly

I am not more than this stream; if you cup me in your hands, you can
    refresh yourself
I can do no work except splash your face
The time for your swim has come…

You sink your head under the water and search out my eyes by holding
    your breath
You press your lips against my closed eyes and I remember

my wolf's life, my scorpion's life, my python's life
my killer's life and the life of hiding in the forest
Once I promised to kiss you and after eons I have come to keep
    that promise
Now nobody will come here, only your head will move in my lap

Again we'll search out one another, the life of this noon in the pressure
    of your lip
This noon is a still stream, under this stream we will lie together
We will not sleep, we will not wake
we will not die and we were never born

Because in this stream time has stopped – because

now we are making love

Translated by Skye Lavin and Joy Goswami

THE LAKE OF THE MOVING LIGHTS

Do not take me along the flow, the winds
have borne my body into the lake of moving lights
Do not take me into darkness, I remember
those exalted moments, falling into the blue pit…
                            I remember still
you sending me down the mine-shaft, but I
could never surface with the casket of jewels
                        held between my teeth
You unclasped the golden sheath from my spine,
                        gilded anew, and I
lying on the moldy earth – rotting, Night-tide
took me by the hand, quite wasted, and the winds
carried my body to the lake of the moving lights
A huge goldfish stays there, he who begot me
I made my way through rocks and tortoise shells–
crawling all the way to the beach and fled the place–
and yet, today, she'll come running, roiling the waters,
when her whole body dazzles in the sun,

I will take the plunge
right into her mouth, for this last time–
                    O Night-tide
That's when you'll find
half of my body inside her mouth
the other half, still in the deep, swimming…

Translated by Chitralekha Basu

EX-HUSBAND

Does he leave for the office on time?
Does he eat properly in the evening?
Does he carry his lunchbox?
Or does he eat in the canteen?

Who washes his clothes for him?
Who makes the tea like before?
What time does Dugga's mother come?
I had to get up early every morning.

Does he still wear that shirt?
That gaudy blue?
That was his choice
I had chosen olive.

Which road does he take home?
Turning left from the shop
the Shiva temple, from the window
I could see the rickshaw stop.

Does he come home straight from the office?
Or does he go straight to his friends
card playing friends, damned friends
Do his friends still come?

The tablecloth on the floor
ash scattered all around the room

the glass rolls the bottle rolls
Staggering he goes to bed

But the bottle breaks and
enters his foot and there is blood
He is unaware then
Who's going to bother in the middle of the night?

Why, that girl.
The one he used to walk with then.
Which girl? That girl?
She moved on long ago.

Oh, good, serves him right.
Who'd clear up the mess?
That the girl wasn't right
I'd seen from the start.

Then who is with him now?
His brother and sister-in-law? Mother, siblings.
There was no one he could call his own
Now he is alone.

Who serves his meals then?
Who wakes him early?
Who lets him in at night?
Who shoulders the burden?

In whose bed does he sleep, then?
Who takes the beatings now?

Who takes the beatings now?

Translated by Indranee Ghosh

ASHES

Still asleep, I know you will come and
stand by my bed. I know, too, you'll first

slowly open those two windows and stand
before the wind to cover the trembling candle.

And when you step out the door
to light the moon in the stillness
and fireflies in the trees–
I'll slip softly out of my skin

to stand alone in the night garden.
In the shadow of the liquid light,
I'll see deer herds rushing through the forest.
On their long horns, won't gold glitter brightly?

Yes, it will. And the scrape of their hooves will spark
diamonds everywhere. I'll run to grab them up.
Suddenly, at dawn, I'll wake and notice
someone burned them, leaving ashes in my room.

I'll cover myself with those ashes, won't I?

Translated by Hassanal Abdullah with Stanley H. Barkan

IN THE EVENING SADNESS COMES

In the evening, sadness comes and stands by the door, his face
hidden, from the dying sun he took colors and painted his body
Sadness comes in the evening,
I stretched my hand and he caught my wrist, in an iron clasp
He pulled me out from my room, I couldn't see
his face, he is ahead of me and I follow him
I cross from the evening to the night, from night to dawn, then
            morning, noon, day, month
crossing water, tree, boat, city, hill, crossing blows,
stumbling, poison, suspicions, jealousy, graves, genocide,
the bones and ribs of civilization, swamp and grass
Then crossing my own death, death after death, going on and on
            My bony fingers holding nothing but a pen
Nothing…

Translated by Skye Lavin and Joy Goswami

THINGS RECALLED AT NIGHT

All that rainfall
Laid out in the rainfall, all those dead bodies.
Beating at the dead bodies, all that wind.
Trembling with the wind but not billowing out,
                all those all-covering shrouds.
Thrusting their muzzles in, tugging at the cloth,
                all those night-time dogs.
Shouting, driving the dogs away, all those attendants
Half-naked, squatting attendants.
Laid down beside the attendants, all those wooden staves
Those clay pipes not burning in the rain
Those not-burning pyres
Spaced apart, all those not-burning pyres

Behind the pyres, the ragged riverbank
and on all those ragged edges, risen from the water,
all their mothers sit
Their heads covered with uncolored cloth
risen up from the water after long years,
climbed down from the rain,
All their mothers sit like small white bundles
so that at burning time
they can be close to their sons–
At burning time when the dead will remember
                a wife left behind
an only daughter who ran away with her lover
unresolved property and a friend's treachery
The dead man will remember the first day at school, and
unseen for so long,
                unprotested, the cause of his own death
When he tries, flustered, to sit up on the pyre
                one last time
and the attendant's stave strikes hard,
                breaking him, laying him out–
Then she can touch that fire-burnt skull
With her age-old kitchen-weary pot-scrubbing shriveled hand
And, spreading the end of her sari over those molten eyes,
                the widow can say

Don't fret, baba, my son, here I am, here, I'm your mother,
              here, right at your side!

Translated by Prasenjit Gupta

VICTORIOUS

I'd traveled a full year past forty when, without
warning, Ember appeared, black staff in hand.
He said: From now on all you'll have is your body.
You'll wander around, smile sweetly, crack jokes,
chatter at the office, put on a crown, turning left
and right so the light shines on your face just so.
But from now on Fire has left you.
He's arrived in the Land of Melancholy. He's bewildered.
He's lost his spark.

On one side of Ember, vast waters. On the other side,
a scorched desert.
A raven is sitting on Ember's head.
That's who put out the flame.

I said: But I still
have so much writing left. I need
to talk with Fire. Where is he?
Ember said: Over there.
Ember points toward a mountain.
Melancholy Mountain.
Fire sits in a cave beneath it, chin resting on his fist.
Grass has grown over his shoes, up to his thighs. Roots dangle
from the muscles of his broad back and arms. Prickly vines
are snagged in his hair and beard. His gaze is empty.
No use trying to talk with him.

As I come out, I see Ember waiting like a sentry,
black staff in hand, ocean on one side, wasteland
on the other. White cloth down to his knees. Shaved head.
The raven is sitting on his head.
It said: Hand over your pen and go away.

But they aren't acquainted with poets. The raven is made
of stone. I grab it and replace it
with a live cuckoo.
So what will you do this time?

That's when it happened. The cuckoo called out,
flapped its wings twice, rose
from Ember's feet to his head,
and springtime caught fire.
Like a madman it spun round and round
with heart-rending cries of delight. And
Fire thrust himself out of the mountain with a groan,
standing tall, hands on his hips, and started
rocking back and forth, toppling the peak into the water.
Then a mermaid floated up, sailed her slender craft
to shore, raced through the sand,
a desert woman covered with a white veil . . . and that's how
I left them – let them do what they like – but
after perching on my head for a long time,
writing is beating its wings, we're ready now
to go back to the cave…

Translated by Carolyn B. Brown

SCHOOLGIRL ON THE VERGE OF VANISHING

What has the girl figured out?
"Uncle" Raju is her mother's lover.

What has the girl heard?
Her mother's cries of passion.

What has the girl been given? Her birthday?
Tight pants, her favorite dish–a cousin's leer.

She's sifted through her class notes, "suggestions"–
she's scaled a mountain of books

exams, exams before her – studying day and night–
a dark room beside her

in the dark she's heard muffled fighting, tooth and nail,
her mother and father tearing each other apart.

Translated by Carolyn B. Brown

DAYABARI HOSPITAL - ANOTHER DREAM

Dayabari Hospital,
wild shrubs on cemented porch,
wilderness within, sand-filled well, broken bricks,
trees growing out of windowsills
and floors, birds, abandoned beds;
I, Kutu, Ghunti, and a brother of hers, Kanu,
playing hide-and-seek here
in this hospital
abandoned since the war.

Seek, hide, seek, hide,
Ghunti's mother calls her inside…
Coming!…
Trees, bricks, birds, a well, sand and lime,
Kutu and I hiding
squatting on our haunches,
the well there,
Kanu searching for us,
us searching each other,
groping…
'Show! Come on, show!'
'No, no,
All right, look, look at this,'
'Ooh!'… just playing…
'Hee, hee, he, sshh! Play? O.K.?'
Whispers – the game went on–

And now
there comes Kutu
out of that hospital
holding her daughter's hand
searching for me; and

Where am I? Me?
I'm sitting on my haunches inside the well,
then I'm coming out of the well
shrubs on my back,
weeds on my arms,
twigs and branches on my head,
'Kutu! Look! Your daughter!...'

Hands tearing at the weeds, hurting,
Hey, hey! Climbing
up my body...to the topmost branch...
Hey, you'll fall...watch it!

Translated by Indranee Ghosh

A BATHROOM FAIRYTALE

Lay yourself down, when you wish to be born lay yourself down
in a grassy field meadow pasture lay yourself down, say Ma Baba Ma Baba
Soon your body will become so tiny in the morning
those work-bound will see on the grass drops of dew
you, a dewdrop, will vanish with the warmth of the sun, go,
go, if you wish to be born, say to the clouds Ma Baba Ma Baba
The clouds will hurl you from their wombs such rain such rain such rain
Down below a beautiful girl enters her roofless rented bath
Today there isn't enough tap water, when suddenly the rain comes
What joy as she folds you to her bosom, such love such love such love...

Translated by Oindrila Mukherjee

DON'T WAIT FOR YOUR LOVER ANY MORE

Dusk has fallen. Go home.
Don't wait any more.
        Trees, flats, trees, signboard, trees
Between them the slate sky – in the distance, shops by evening
        every scooter and Maruti car
flashes light and turns by the culvert.

The same storm that came and went seven days ago
is coming back again.
       On the street dust swirls with paper bags,
the wind's voice gradually rises to a roar.
       What a strange restlessness
has begun to ripple through the suburban pond's water…

Go home, wait no more. Go and see,
the child you left behind with the nanny
fell asleep on the floor while playing
in a jungle of toys big and small.

Translated by Oindrila Mukherjee

BATHING

I do not know how to put it: come, charm me, this
                                    one time
I've looked from afar, always. Never revealing my thoughts
never thought I could summon the courage to go,
                        drown myself in that fall–
but today, I felt my time running out, fast…

I know, brute force is all you expect of men
Your lover, he'd promised to take you to flower country
but left you on the way, I know his promises,
wrapped around your hair, even now, a garland of dead bones.

But what if I tell you, I'm the one who's come, asking to
knock that knotted carcass off your hair?
I'm the one for whom you've preserved
your eager river, still whole, all these years.

I step out at night – hiding my burnt-out wings
from this civil world, even now.
Comatose and sick, all through my youth. I saw
a flower come to life, sitting beside the dead man's cot.
Even now, at this late hour, I don't let the desert sleep
so that the girl, born blind, might feel the moonbeams…

Look, the desert night, sending signals from eye to eye
if you got the message, come, charm the poet
                                    who cannot hear
and, if he's cowering, gouge his eyes
in full public view, pour your kisses, frozen long since
                            in those burnt-out eyes
Let the world watch, right here, under the glaring sun
and the polite people on the street, stunned
as you bathe, out in the open, under the waterfall,
                                    a mad poet by your side...

Translated by Chitralekha Basu

"IF YOU ASK ME"

> *If you ask me, "what have you done with your life"*
> *then I must tell you...*

One day I vomited, one day I swallowed
One day I touched the water and it changed into milk
One day by looking at me an *apsara* lost herself
One day without telling me both my hands flew away in the wind

One day I hid in a drunkard's stomach as a strong drink
The next day I came out, in another way entirely, as the tears of a
    beautiful woman
at once the muslin handkerchief sucked me in consoling, consoling

One day I beat her
One day I kicked her
One day I stuck out my tongue
One day I lathered myself with soap
One day I lathered her
If you don't believe me, go and ask your wife.

One day I managed only caw, caw
One day I took on the scarecrow
One day I adopted a pig, oh yes, one day a goat

27

One day I played a flute, oh yes one day for Radha I played
One day I pressed my face into a woman's lap
while the rest of me fell to someone else
If you don't believe me, go and ask my fate...

One day my body was filled with green leaves
and my fingers were long white lilies
and my hair was a cumulus cloud—
when the wind comes, it will float anywhere
One day I was the grass in field after field,
but only because you come and pour your body into it
yes, my eyes exceed all that is permitted
they roam from river to river to river

On the river Ganges I lay my body down, like a small bridge
so people can go from this side to that, no passports
From one side came Asgar Ali Mandl and Babul Islam
from that side to this came your own mother once,
a teenager in her first sari, and your aunt Santi in a frock

While writing the Constitution of the nation, I got a bit sleepy
In that moment someone came and scribbled on it: oh, oh I want to
    make her

One day running out in the main street naked
I submitted this year's national budget
One day I opened my mouth and one day
I shut it
In my yes-saying mouth there was no food
and in my no-saying mouth there was no food.
One day blood dripped down my cheeks
I looked for my torn-out eyes in the water and the mud of a paddy

One day a knife stabbed me in the back
I collapsed into the yard before the hut, coughing blood
The village crowd came to see me, their lanterns held up

One day body ablaze, I leapt from a burning hut into a pond
The next morning I was surprised to see it in the newspapers
I got excited, tears fell, I called people, sweat dripped from my forehead
I kept the collected sweat in my file cabinet

If anybody comes to do research in the future
they can set the papers on fire, burn many people

Kill! Kill! Kill!
Different ways for men and women
Kill! Kill! Kill!
Beat them till their hearts come out their mouths
Kill! Kill! Kill!
Beat them till their babies come out of their wombs
Kill! Kill! Kill! Kill! Kill-l-l-l!…

In this place we must use screams
that break the skull into small pieces
In this place we must use such intercourse
half the body will be buried in the earth
and turn quickly into coal
In this place we must spit
so that when it comes from the mouth, it explodes like stars
In this place we must use a song,
in which the hero and heroine will fly in the sky
and their hands, legs, head, and sex will be ripped away – all from a song

Every limb will cry out for every other limb
Each limb will caress the other limb
At last not knowing what to do next
and they will return to how they were
Here such a kiss must be used
So that the last letter of "kill"
And the last letter of "help"
Are torn away
By an immense centripetal force
They will run toward each other
They will try to be one
And those lovers apart for eternities
Will turn their face up to the sky
Their lips open in that sound,
That last "l", the "p"
And they will be silent

If you ask me today, "why have you written lies in hundreds of lines?"
If you ask, "why haven't you learned yet the duty of a poet?"

I will lecture about "a particle"
I will say I was born from a particle of sand
I was born from a grain of salt
and the unknown unnamed drop of rain
that watched me from a leaf on a high tree branch
and then fell near me
I know nothing more than this

If you ask me today, in what labyrinth,
in what black hole, in what hidden drains of the nation
I wander, in what armory do I drink a cup of tea,
against what billboard, on what flyover,
do I smash my head,
what deer came and nuzzled my foot,
what swan prayed to me to come and twist her neck

Then I will say: Over the clouds, over the cloud, over the clouds
in thousands and thousands of drops of rain
I jump and dance over fields and cities

If you ask me today,
Are there buds on your plant?
Are you Shundillo or Bhardwaj?
Are you Durlov or Koiborto?
Are you battery or cashbox?
Are you mango tree or banana?
Are you in shoes or sandals?
Are you Muslim or Chandala?
Are you a dead lingam or are you alive?

Then I will tell you the story of that night,
that night on the calm grass
from the ground quietly, quietly, quietly
mud and stones burst, and a long minaret
spun out and vanished into the black heaven
from the long fire tail in the sky
I jumped arms spread into the whirling foam womb of time

Now I am in the last ocean of the distances and the iron wheel revolves
    under the water

Now I am at the very beginning of the ocean and the iron wheel revolves
     under the water
All body and all bodiless awaken to the rough burst of life through me

I am cutting through time's current now, I reach in two directions, past
     and future
I am a monstrous fish lashing my tail, the waterspout in the ocean rises
     and falls
a fountain springs from my nose in a burning cloud

A rope is fastened to the sword on my nose
The other end of the rope goes on and on, up
to where there's no earth, no solar system
to where the dark ether wave swells with stars and cosmic dust
There from one galaxy's island to another
a lifeboat of flame floats floats swings swings

Apart from that
I have nothing else to say

Translated by Skye Lavin and Joy Goswami

SCIENTIST

> *"If I knew the Germans would not succeed in constructing the bomb,
> I would never have lifted a finger." Albert Einstein*

Five pages I wrote, the last time,
on the end that is death
That done, I moved far away
my earnings seemed spent

But just how far was it
I knew, from the ocean
and the same law will tell you
the sun, is, after all, the sun

Three pages I wrote, on the sun
and everything under it

of which a line I shall leave
to his children – a vile lot

Made more vile with each death
and so the earning and spending goes on
I'm yet to include a chapter on
the distant seas

Translated by Chitralekha Basu

THE WAY I WRITE

There's so much that you know, Young Poet,
you'll give a few leads, now and then, won't you?
Blind and helpless each time I start
my hands, cupped together for a gulp of water
get shredded and torn, wash away with the flow

I keep swimming, swimming after them
I'm gasping for breath
Thorns stick to my body, I bang my head
until I slave and sweat, and get my hands back

I reach the shore, spread a scroll out on the sand
Writing done, I go for a wash in the sea
but my hands, the vile twosome, deceive me again
They float, washed away, far away in the sea

Once again, I run, run along the sandy shore…

Translated by Chitralekha Basu

THE STORYTELLER

Ash roams around the room, printed in darkness
Paper, book, cover, picture, a dead bird's call–
Ash roams around the room, held down underneath it
one chest full of tales seeks to shoot up through the floor.

You can't help it, you are a storyteller
One day you had been a part of those tales
grasping your throat you have strangled again and again
the scream of delight when death was happening...

Was death happening? Or does death not come?
It comes, it advances, it retreats, no last moments
This heart-breaking strain of pleasure is strange, unknown
You have never been whipped this way before.

What happened in the end? When after an eternity
on one heart another's dying lips
overflowed limitless blue, the sky breaking descended in the room
The grieving, devastated storm rolls about the floor

But you are restless, so there's no peace, none–
the fire's not coming down, the fire doesn't lower its face!
Where will it drop the lightning, where ought it to drop, it is

this anxiety that makes the cloud beat its head against the skies
Where is the tree? That which can calmly take the lightning?
One tree and another and another for
this test it has burnt, in the scorched darkness
Ash roams around the room, paper, book, picture...

The cover on the book, beneath, the dead bird's call
The lightning wanders in the air, says, 'Will you be my tree?'
What? Again? The floor cracks – gapes
A chest full of tales shoots up through the floor, poet!

Translated by Indranee Ghosh

FROM SUJYOPORA CHHAI

<u>Page 16</u>
Black grass on violence
bones under, earth-stopped skull

No one is to know

Holding to my mouth the round earth like a basin
Throwing out from inside the bones, earth, coal oil, iron
into that empty skull all night long
Loudly hacking I spit blood, gouts of blood

The sky flows beneath.

Page 20
Death? Why, he comes and sits on the window
an earthen cup in his hand. As he sips
down his transparent throat descend
molten nebulae, flattened sun, droplets of moon
over his veins and arteries
starts to flow the whole Milky Way.

When he goes away from the window
tumbling in the currents of smoke come into the room
the past – a knotted lump – the future like a lump.

Page 21
What an inaccessible moon is strung alongside your boat!
On the other side what a beautiful boatman!
Whose face is of a skeleton, whose arms are of rusted iron
Tell, tell your boatman to begin beating with iron.
The invaluable moon, it, too, is willing to break cheaply!
Falling in the water in pieces, the water spurts up near and far…

Say, don't you want to stand in that scene again

when moving aside the waters to eat the comets
the demon fish mouth of the water god floats up?

Page 24
Each time I am cut
will be found animal blood. On the mountain top
if I am hung upside down
the birds will scream - the sky will turn red

In the waters of the ocean
my buffalo head with crooked horns
will be seen in place of the sun.

Page 25
Rising to go towards the past
are battle corpses, thousands and thousands

Snow on the mountain crest

Behind them with lamps lit
sit little cottages

Families with lost husbands and sons.

Page 39
Having killed his own son,
look, there goes the needy

Having sold her own daughter
the mother returns
on their way back, from their store fall
sand instead of tears, coins and discs of blood – round
After that all is water. Only on those rounded rocks
the fire will blaze one day, and striding into that fire
or a land drowned in rage, sorrow and fire
again, searching the madman stalks.

Page 57
The idiot sits in the field
a mountain on his head.
Earth on his plate, grass.

He eats digging into the plate–
going down in layers like curd in a pot–
his hunger isn't quenched – the wealth of the mine
diminishes – grows less – in a slurp
the womb of oil is emptied

His hands full of mud-gravy, the idiot
drums on the bottomless earth
mistaking it for his plate.

Page 60
That is the river of time. I

dip my hands
from the cemented bank
My finger melts. Wrist, arm
melt. With a head on my shoulders
I am the armless and legless *Jagannath*.
I sit
on the back of a spinning ball with traceries of rivers and stream
I whirl in the void.

Page 69
Ocean? Or an ancient python? Having swallowed the world

It sleeps
The gaping cavity of its mouth
is dark. The roar of waves
That is the way
the whole living world unwittingly enters
On the verge of that wood
Leaning against a tree at the moment of your death
Looking into the glowing eyes of that python
After all this time
you see that it is blind. The eyes are of pebbles
They glitter in the moonlight
You see that the roar of the waves is really
a tongueless sound
You see that the cavity of its mouth
is boundless black but a star or two float in it.

Translated by Indranee Ghosh

FROM MOUTAT MAHESWAR

1.
I will go out soft from the house
I will go from language into a bird
rising smoke from murderer and firing squad far below me will shrink
I will see wrecking on the distant earth
your giant carriage of revenue.

10.
Go once again, buy once more some profound saying,
the trader despairs–
the time to speak advances – it comes, it comes, it's come
Do not hold back
Open up, speak out, don't be smothered by the burden
of twisted ever-secret tales
Breaking hard on the shore of conscience is wave upon wave of reticence.

16.
This book will guard from many storms
This book has risen from deep waters
The water and storm are not much really
to catch the lightning this book is the sky-kissing post at the far end of
     the field
Beneath it, dusk
red and blue spoon and ladle
djinn, fairy
fox, crane.

19.
Whenever I ride the sky the kite comes
thinks of me as kin
Birds fly touching my body.

Taking me for a white coil of wispy cloud
one or two aeroplanes
break in through my chest and break out through my back.

And yet you want to know my age, my tree?
Would you like to know my address?
Which little alley? Wind number. What?
Do I even know how many bridges stretch across me?
Still fly somewhere wings that I have made?

Translated by Indranee Ghosh

23.
My palm burnt with blue – how splendid to see!
I'd dipped my hand into the sky – he, he, heee!

Translated by Joy Goswami and Indranee Ghosh

24.
My mother had short hair, couldn't even make a bun.

So I entered her eyes
and all day
I'd lie around there reading books.

What incomprehensible books! Hard red trees turn into breath!
In the end even Ma would not breathe.

Those eyes today a hundred thousand times
wider have I spread over the whole land.
So I say, don't look at any old time below any old water
Eyes shut tight, browless, hands and legs curled up, bald-headed
a human embryo within the trembling fingers of fern
sways just a little – how many smaller and bigger fish bend past it
No one pecks.

Rising all around him
the roaring prayer of fire.

Translated by Indranee Ghosh

TALE OF A FUNERAL

That day when from out the river of fire
we lifted Ma's body floating
her body in flames, Sister, you remember
suspicion in the neighbours' eyes?

Long beaked, hairs bristling on necks
their veterans advanced
said, `This committee pronounces judgement, listen well –
these here have no right to cremate her.'

That night we fled the village
Ma's body on shoulder, the moon burning overhead
On our path lay a poisonous swamp
On our path lay a quarry of salt and lime.

My fingers have dropped, your breast
has withered with the pungent lime
There was no food, no water to cleanse oneself
We were fully absorbed in our pallbearers' task.

The land we came to had dead trees everywhere
Skins of dead animals hung from their boughs
on the bank of the last river in the world
We have now laid down our mother's skeleton.

Sister, listen, we will not burn her bones
We'll keep them in the crevice of a tree
We haven't learnt. Those who come after,
will they not learn their proper use?

Our bodies are covered with fungus
No eyes, just a crater of burning rage
I have forgotten if ever I was a man
You don't remember when your periods stopped.

On the east is a skeletal light
Behind us drops a dusky darkness
In the middle of the last graveyard of the world
we sit, two thieves of a corpse.

Translated by Indranee Ghosh

FOR A CLOUDGIRL

When as a cloud I used to play
with a group of clouds far away, one day
a little cloudgirl said to me,
'Tell me, boy,
who may you be?'
'I am Puff!' I said.

Angrily she turned to me,
'A lie! Can such a name
ever be?'

'Of course, it can,' I said to her,
'but first you must
listen to my story.'

'No, no,' she begged,
'it's bound to be the same old tale,
the same old queen, the same old king,
the shields and spears and what-have-you,
a prince upon a flying steed–
No please, not that,
that's rot,' she said.

I said, 'But, for you,
I'd write anew.'

'Will you?' she cried,
'Really? Well, it must be long
and, remember, when it's done,
I must have it there from you.'

I said, 'For you
I'd write a whole wide world.'

And so I wrote, and still I wrote,
and happened to fill two or three pages,
when, even before I knew how or what,
I was possessed.

So I went in search
to my old cloudfield,
Not a face was there
that I once knew.

But one was different from the rest.
And it was to her I went.
To her I said, 'Are you the one?
Are you she?
Are you the cloudgirl I once knew?'
'I don't recall,' she replied,
'These things you say, I don't recall.'

'I was supposed to write,' I said,
'Me it was you asked to write.'

'Oh, is it here?' she said to me,
'Throw it in the village pond,
and look,
I'm no more a cloud, you know,
now they call me rain.'

And all at once, there came a shower
soaking me from head to foot
drenching me to my very roots–
and with other rainy winds and rain
in swelling currents, she went away,
melted far away, somewhere…

Far away, far, far away…

'They call me rain,
they call me rain–,'
Saying to myself these words,
in my wet clothes
I sat there waiting
under a tree,
waiting for,
I don't know whom,
perhaps for cloud, perhaps for rain.

And then I saw
another rain
a rain who knew,
who I was and said,
'What's there to be sad about?
Go back and write
once again.
We're in the middle of the monsoon now,
up in our years in work, you know,
in different places, many lands.

You, too,
have work to do
to write once more.
We'll come back,
when work is done
when the rainy season's run.'

To write once more
a whole wide world,
I went away from my old home
and built myself a home anew,
deep in the woods
my pen and I.

Alone I'll live
Alone I'll cook
myself a meal—
a fistful or two
of sand and dust—
Whoever comes to me, I must,
I must write them all.

That fairytale will be mine alone,
the fairytale that dares to dream
a hundred dreams within
a whole wide world.

And so I bent my head to write,
to write all day,
to write all night,
till night, till day
erased themselves
I didn't know where.
And when my hand
grew numb with writing
I stopped then, recollecting
how I'd lost track
of date and month and year.
Looking at my work, I saw,
in trying to write a whole wide world,
not a notebook had I filled.

When suddenly, a downpour came,
on my little notebook fell the rain,
on my whole life's work came the rain,
tumbling in these deepest woods.
Out there, then, beneath the tree
the peacock dances in delight,
from tree to tree there are birds aflight
Birds that say, 'For the poet we are
here in the forest–
here in its midst.
For him, nowhere,
nowhere did we,
admit defeat.'

From his cottage, then, the poet looks
away into that far-off land,
beyond the woods,
beyond the fields,
beyond the river,
Where there will be rain forever;
where no one ever goes,
where none has been before.

And the poet sees that distant land,
where, near the forest spring–
prancing here, prancing there,
a sunshine clouddoe there he sees,
his childhood's golden doe,
once more.

Translated by Indranee Ghosh

FROM "GARMENT OF LEAF"

Everybody is a garment of leaf
Everybody is a handmade flute
Everybody is a longish hat
Everybody, say "I love"

But love may break.

The garment of leaf torn
floating away in stormwaters
knocking against hidden rocks
a couple of flutes, hat, leaf

Store them away for us!
. . . .

On the horizon, where the ocean ends, there
keeping the black rock afloat you
went back with the boat.
After that how many suns have set
How many moons have shown their faces
How many animals that exist in no world, who are
really monstrous huge clouds, who, as they float,
change their forms,
But you never went back. So you never could know,
that stone came alive long ago
It's grown a lot from day to day,
now it's angry,
now as soon as it sees a ship in the distance,
pulls it close to itself,
cracks it on itself scattering all the machinery,
                          instruments, people,
but it can't find you.
When its rage cools,
panting it sees near its shoulder
the burnt face of the moon
in little handfuls the sea is splashing water on it
Cheek by jowl float pyrewood and corpse, rope and
                          torn garment of leaf
and far away
there goes back over the black waters,
goes back how many thousand thousand years,
that boat, your boat...

One day, no star rose in the sky.
So how could I know the way?
So I never went home.

I lay down right there in the field. Just a matter
                              of somehow
lasting one night.
The instant sleep came the field on that side
put out its hand. Trapped finger between finger.
Pulled me. I
rose up on tiptoe walked over to that field,
falling on it, kissing it again and again
descended into some strange grave.
When the spell broke, there was earth on my back,
mounds of earth,
a whole highway on my back

Now, except for staying on in this grave
except for inching ahead with all this on my back
even in this darkness guessing the way ahead,
except for going on writing about that illicit
                              love
there's no other way for me

ADDENDUM

That lover and his love
checking in with a bagful of sleeping pills
                        into a seedy hotel
That young man and that young woman
bottle of Folidol in hand, quietly locking the
                                    door
That boy and that girl
near the railtracks, in the bushes, standing in
                        the evening
                Far away
            the light of the train
Today, tomorrow, the day after, and the next day
                              all of them
will be discovered dead…
They were after all teacher and student,
    husband's brother and brother's wife,
            they were after all distant cousins
They took this road out of the public eye and got
                        away

for good when they left the stuffy hotel room,
        hospital, morgue and railtracks
And rising up
     a little beyond the sky
set up home – yes – by squatter's right.
       There trees are made of cloud
       There cottages are made of air – there
       are leaves, only garments of leaf.
            In that country now
the torn wife is having her picture drawn by
       her torn young lover
Wiping the blood off his lip she is saying:
"Come, Botai, now sing me a song!"
       The youth is mending the autopsy stitches
      all over her body with his touch
And a hot-headed poet,
     looking up from the plain
     is disputing on and on with the gods
that this little bit of heaven be signed over
        to them without delay.

Translated by Probir Ghosh

HUNTSMAN, DESIST

The silence cracks, the dust curls up
Clouds merge into the column of dust
The universe whirls, the furnace roars
The sun is all but swallowed up

Not the sun, it is the doomsday moon
The raven flies off, the moon in its beak
That's the moon the madman's arrow struck
The madman we know the hunter

In ancient time that life caught in love's act
destroyed by arrow and by spear
The dying curse still has the power to harm
The moon still waxes and wanes, year to year

From ancient warring times the tug goes on
to snatch and eat the food from other mouths
Thin bodies clad in bark, quilt and rag
Overhead, the sun's hot pan, frying

Drying in the sand, floating in the sea
the dead and hurt, broken chariot, dead horse
clutching their weapons, faces hid in grass
Two men, two neighbors they had been

The neighbor's land, let it be all mine
The neighbor's village, let it do my will
The neighbor king, let his tribute come to me
My weapons let my neighbors strike with awe

Do neighbors live in this same world?
In their space and in their sunlit waters
If I ask you today to spread poison
you'll make sure it happens, won't you?

That plot, playing catch with skill
thought up in guarded chambers
Technology, talent, science steal
quietly on their belly to dig a hole

In the pit a furnace, the flames roar
The fire rises above ground just here
The ashes make an umbrella in the sky
There is no way whatever to escape

Like pebbles the birds drop in flocks
Poisoned water leaps onto land
For a thousand miles atoms turn to ash
For a thousand miles the forests burn

Burnt hut, crushed bone, brick and wood
rubble heaped like stupas on the public path
crumbled soil, burnt crop meadows
People are dead in offices, homes, on roadside

People have died, and more and more are born
Twisted limbs, bodies all deformed–
some mouths with no tongue, some legs with no bone
Who's that crawling like a beast on all fours?

The poison mixes with the seed of loins
Women and crops are lost in turn
The helicopter spins around and growls
There's no trace of radioactivity.

What year were you born, O man of science?
And what year you, O government man?
Have children been born into your house?
Are their noses, mouths and arms as they should be?

What do we have left for future births?
A little, sheaves of grain, grass
the bird helped from earth to branch
There is the song of Nanak, Tulsidas

Through the charred village Tulsiji walks on
From the pier Kabir the weaver sings
Yet the Shriramacharita lies in tatters on the street
and a red-eyed sadhu open sword in hand

Brother Kabir, who listens to your song?
Who's mad enough to plead, "explain, explain"?
Who are they on the pavement left all night?
Whose child is that crying to be fed?

Which child toils at the tea shop all day long
to earn a living – and the owner's slaps?
Which loving mother lulls her son to sleep
so she can turn tricks all night long?

Their lot, well, let it be as now
Pour out their lives along a different track
Whether they get enough to eat or not
at least I have this weapon in my hands

Weapon in the ground, weapon in flight
Far skies alight in the weapon's glory

The bright weapon's rays strike the water
The Granth Sahib floats by in the river

Into those waters floats Behula's little boat
Lakhindar supine inside the mosquito net
A cripple he is, poisoned by radiation
The little boat stops at every other pier

At each pier an era is standing still
The giant bridge shadows river and sea
The crippled child has bitten into your breast
Whom do you love, child or man?

Having borne the weight of children and of grain
you rest, in stillness, universe
Then the silence cracks, an age rises up
sky worn 'round the head, sceptre held in hand

The broken moon is pierced on the sceptre's point
The ocean is thrashing underfoot
Its shoulders touch the mountain's tall shoulders
Night is all but swallowed up

At dawn the image is not there
The sun worshipper hopes for warmth
The Zend-Avesta open in the sun
 Radiation has stained its pages too

The universe whirls, rivers and mountains too
There's stench of corpses in Lachhmanpur
Jews turn into soil under the soil
The grain sways on mass graves

The sun moves from this land to that
The poor Moslem sits at his namaaz
his white cap the dove of peace
God sups only after he has supped

Some leave sugar grains even by ant hills
Some use a stick to prop the bent sapling
Despite destruction again and yet again
there still rise new waves of plant and beast

Who is a Hindu? Who asks?
In the face of this query, stars collapse
Lighting the oil-lamp after the holy bath
the fasting saint now sits down to eat

All of us we come for nourishment
The bells toll at the village church
The Kerala fisher comes home in his boat
May Mother Mary protect your life

But it's not protection but "defense"
The path that leads to warlike ostentation
Go merge alone into black in Ajanta's chambers
O Padmapani, Awalokiteswar

The lotus drops hard from hand to earth
earth covered with potholes and pits
The desert sand billows fountain like
after the 'Little Buddha' has duly grinned.

Poison from the earth seeps into crops
O women it enters you each one
No matter where you are, you're infertile
You lay it all at the feet of gods

The lover's arms are spread out on the earth
The arms have fissures, houses cracked in ruins
Cracked stone figurine of Parswanath
On the ground the Tirthankars all laid out

With the moon in its beak the raven flies
Weapon of doom, it's really not a moon
For ages, the huntsman's kept the bowstring drawn
Push the button and the earth will burst

Come, poet, resist – Huntsman, desist,
Say it and let the termite hill break
Let sun and moon stand on each side of day
Let the old images burn inside the cave

Look how night flows on Ganga's banks
See how the boatman punts the Padma barge
Hear how the things you and we say
are transformed by Bhatiali song

See there the dust storm's died out
See, having swum through moonlight the dove of peace
comes back to rooftop, pecks grain in the yard
Maize and grain from the fields on which we sweat

There, there the night flows on the Jamuna bank
There, there have come our Shyam and our Rai
There, don't you hear, sitting in the ruined shrine
our Meerabai is still singing of love

Is it so easy to destroy us all?
The nightly cycle turns on our feet
Long after Mahabharat we have come
We have come across much space and time

Huntsman, having come into your weapon's range
let our village turn to dust, to ash
From that heaped mound of ashes
weapon-free it arises, we can see

Beyond it, the ocean swells
Before it in the cloud the lightning flashes

It has twisted your arm in the water
wrenched the weapon away and into the water

There in the water the sun goes down

Against a nearby hill the wave knocks its head

Beyond the wave the sun goes down

The century turns – the sun goes down

Translated by Probir Ghosh

ESSAY CONCERNING LIGHT

1. Today again after many years, to discover
                'a technique to revive the dead'
Today again after many years, to plug one's ears
                        and sleep
Again after many years to sit at home memorizing
                Bande Ali Mian's rhymes
Today again after many years, inspiration on
                seeing a green bathroom
and being commissioned to write the biography
                        of a cloud
Today again to shoulder the *shiuli* tree cut down
                long ago and
bring it home and grow treefuls of flowers
And lying under the tree at dead of dawn
to try to spell 'flowerbed' again, today after
                        many years
to end all quarrels with the cuckoo,
to cut off illicit relations with the fragrant
                flower, and
today again, though agitators from field
                and rallyground still
call to arms, simply to walk away and not give a
                        hoot
and to let them know that.
Every Monday a fortress opens up in front of me
and inspiration walks inside it lamp in hand

Inspiration's shadow falls to the ground,
                her long robe trails
The old cannon come rolling down, and in rasping
                        voice,
after cautioning the colorful about this,
                        turning
this scene around backwards with a push again
Again to print pictures of autumn on all the skies
I let loose springtime on plant and leaf
to fill Bengal after Bengal to the brim with
                        rainy season

52

Standing in paper boats one after another
                         waving hands
going to Gangasagar again after many years
because it's just today that the lid having
                         come off
smoke and fire start to come out of my head
Save yourselves

2.   Just now I was writing about the *shiuli* tree and
that instant one came into the room
Her name is
       "A branch to keep waves on"
Oh but it's neither wave nor branch
Her name is
       "I've made colors"

Just now I was writing about applying colors
This instant the one who came out of my room
Her name is
       "Please take a bath, sir"

Oh it's not bath nor room at all
Her name is
       "In the quiet of the waterfall"

Just now I was writing about waterfalls and
that instant the one who covered my page with her
                         hand
Her name is
       "Caress me"

Ah who says it's either caress or hand
Her name is
       "Red flare blue flare"

Just now I was writing about two kinds of flare
and the cloud came darkening my page and said
Everyone wants to hear something from you on the
                         subject of sunlight
Today's Monday, you can start right away…

3.   Today when I'm having to write for ordinary people
an essay concerning sunlight
The essay concerning shadow is lying behind all
        those tall buildings and below tall trees
When the essay concerning motion has started
                running even before dawn
on the heads of porters and backs of rickshaw-vans
And when the essay concerning vapor is puffing
                intermittently in rage
under the lid of the pot cooking rice
And the essay concerning sound is roaring through
    big car's motorhorns, middleclass pressure cookers
the Shiva-temple bells and government siren-cars
And my essay concerning air with a heighhh-ohh
shout belches out of a tubewell-drilling Joginder
And my essay concerning high temperatures is
                shooting out
through the eyes of the conductor just slapped by
                a passenger
And the essay concerning earth is coming up shovel
                by shovel
going on basket by basket to fill up marshland
And the essay concerning water without a word to
                anyone
goes on sucking the sleeve of the young lady's
                kameez
and also leaping in joy
'Long life to you' – the open-mouth roadside pipes
And dancing too, the essay concerning water has
                started to dance
in time with the street-kids' splash-splash-jig…
And then a wave of light is hitting me from
                behind
pushing me on beyond day and night

4.   Dense black and dark
the womb
Choking hot or cold, solid or liquid
the womb

Inside it stirred my
fetal state
piercing the surface rising upwards from the
                earth's center it began
My autobiography
cracking layer after layer of rock with its head
suddenly diving, helplessly tossing in water
being forged in a stream of hot metal
upwards piercing the soil or downwards came my
        autobiography, not knowing from which side
                of the globe it would come out
Parting
earth and sand and earth and sand and earth
Parting
the skull and helmet, not yet turned to earth,
a handful of dead hair stuck on the skull
Within sand the whispering of secret murders long
                                ago
and within earth, the ceaseless sobbing of
                        moldering queens
broken goblets and broken down baths and crawling
through holes in bones of buried soldiery of both
                                sides,
and parting parting parting those turned to earth
in their thousand thousand families and
And piercing the earth
my autobiography raised its head in a desert
and again I entered the limits of day and night

5.   This doesn't mean that just by groping in the
                        sand heap
you'll find its whereabouts
This doesn't mean that it has hidden its face
This doesn't mean that you'll be able to touch
                even a hair of its head
        This doesn't mean that it's forgotten
                how to butt with its head
This does mean that,
it still lies half submerged in the desert

Blazing daily in the sun
and goes wild with each conflagration, upsets the
                    atmospheric layers
finds no shore from ocean to mountain range
It means
this poem is fire that poem is lightning and
that other poem is the south-west monsoon wind,
                    that
when it blew across my country
left little Mou in the house across the street
who morning and evening goes book in hand to learn
                    to type
from typing to singing class and Shumi has ended
                    up
as far away as Nagerbazar, flat of chest, morning
                    and evening
tutoring, acquiring no lover, till suddenly
it happened, one evening, with me
We lost all sense of direction
Floating floating we ended up in mid-ocean
and the instant we came she tore away
from on top of me into space a meteor
And having become a broken piece of ship's timber
                    floating floating floating floating
I came aground where
                    habitation begins
All day I lie by the water and dry
and when evening falls
and one by one the lights go on
                    in the houses
I get up, I stand up as if I were alive
in front of the windows one by one – see the
                    children at study
I ask, will Teacher come today?

6.   Then one day light enters
through windows one by one
through the upstairs gallery through the rooftop
                    garret

through the streetpost also through the lamp
   above the street food the light advances
Checks to see if my muscles have withered to the
     right twist
whether or not the spine has smelted to proper
     strength
and at once transmutes me into fuel
and I start a prayer:
Break me, stick me into the bottom of a
     brick-piled stove
May the pavement people be happy
Chop me up, mix and burn with all the dry
leaves, on winter nights let my country people
     warm
their hands and feet
Then pull me out, pull me out from the firepit and
     toss the long embers
shack by shack may your neighbors' households
burn to ashes. Great.

7.   Great, how dandy your run over the fire now
To escape the fire
running, running, hands and back warding off
   arrows, catching arrows on the fly,
preludes for each new mayhem and the blood-
     chilling
substance of painful shrieks
You understand how fine your getaway,
you artist shedding blood all the way,
hullabaloo baloohulla muted cursing
  sounds of weeping, the last breath exhaled
    Trampling trampling on, your run
leaping up underfoot, entrapping the feet, the
    bite of all these fluid flames
Who says, who says so, from under the running
    the ghost of the swamp says so,
They've buried me, ripped open my gullet, the
    knife is in the pond
it says, Here's my navel opened up and my entrails

in pieces, spreading as fertilizer from plot to
                                    plot
                            The crop
sways, Can you recognize me I'm the sharecropper's
ghost there's no need to redeem me
The daily murder over who gets what, trouble over wives,
                    men cut up over cutting crops
                            Blood
                        Bloodshed
All blood, all innards, all heads, all bones, all
                    calcium, all phosphate
under the paddy, under the jute, pressing and
                        pushing up the paddy crop
The seedling stirs and roars, the fire burning
the soles of your feet makes them new again and
                            mixing freely
with this earth-substance I enjoy possession
                        of my land
                    So who said
under the soil it's only darkness?

8.   Today it's a darkness, tomorrow it's a fire, the day after
a hair-tossing
wave
Inside the wave a something or other

Possibly a peak, which has begun to form last
                                    night
and the sea is sloping away on both sides

On a rock am I, a plant just awake from sleep

A gust of wind
            a cyclone
a cloud, clouds jostling
a black
            a black column
sounds inside the column, landslides inside the
                            column

and right up to the horizon a collapse
a spill reaching up to the sky
After that all things sink away

By the shoreline I, a life, have just opened my
eyes

A distance, after that
water, after that water, after that distance,
after that distance, after that
water
a flicker, a color, a circle, a
day, a wave

I leap on to the head of the wave
a tiny fish

Tiny fish, tiny fish, one fish, two fishes,
three fishes, shoal after shoal leaping,
dropping to the water, one day not dropping
One flew on, flew on, with wing and
feather, flew on out there where there's sight of
the shore

9.   Where is this shore?
In the middle of water.
Who sleeps beneath the water?
I.

Many miles from this shore
in the night from the water rises
my reptile face.
My neck is like a column. From my
eyes' empty sockets sandy water
Many kinds of fish and slime
roll out and drop below. Like an eyeless camel's
the face, neck twisting around for a look back,
many miles back, towards its back,
the vegetation that has taken on life
the birds asleep

and all living things

Looks, then the gigantic face set on its column
drops once more into the sea

10.   –Hey wait, you can't have the right
to say just anything.
Or license to see just anything
or passport to write just anything.
There's a science to everything. This time
you're really, really going beyond the limit

–Okay, but the room I come to work in
it's a ghouls' workshop. Set on a raft, this room
has come swaying swaying to shore one day, now
its stone walls are pocked with all kinds of
holes. From one of them appears
an artist's brush come alive and towards it
colors rush of their own.
And of its own a mural stands up and stands
against the wall. In some holes are
big fat books. The stories of their own
come walking out of the books,
and even after the book is finished walk on
wherever they wish. From some holes
roll down great rocks and the roof cracking
Lightning strikes it again and again.
Splinters flying, of its own it turns now
                    into a face,
now into the branch of a tree and now into female
                    sculpture,
then it flies out through the hole in the roof.
                    And
instantly before me
someone takes the great ocean lying supine
and stands it up vertical reaching out to sky,
the ocean is then all fire instead of water,
the sky can't be seen at all, only on all sides
thousands, thousands of small and large lumps are
shooting out, the fire-ocean at one point

pulls me in too, and spills me out and up
beyond the fountain above its head
that very instant once again I violate
the limits of day and night…

Aa aa aa aa aa…who are you, who are you, what
                                        are you
which are you, you are color, lava color, comet
                    color, scorched red
diamond color, heat is white, heat is all, where
                    am, in what world
how many suns am I passing, arms made of
                    particles, legs made
of particles, all a whirlpool, all spiraling,
                    floating colors, blind colors,
I don't know their names, heat is pure, heat is
                    all, in it an egg
transparent egg, floating, running, egg, ovum, egg
                    of creation
inside, that eyes-shut-fingers-clenched, I am I,
inside the egg opening the eyes, opened the eyes,
                    just this instant
My my
fetal state…

On the other side, left behind under the volcano
my brain is humming in joy,
and in the earth's cavernous center my hot heart
                    is throbbing
and my smoking autobiography, up from the desert
roams the habitations, takes part in
Coining axioms, makes musical instruments out of
                    wood
Aims weapons, raises the mouthful
to the mouth, snaps fingers, whistles a tune,
with both hands conquers lack and want, builds
love anew, finds union, and coming home
late at night drenched by rain, sees as she
                    opens the door,
in his mate's eyes, a light…

And my essay concerning light is then
rushing on shooting past star after star after
                    nebula into a dark open mouth...

Translated by Probir Ghosh

PART AUTOBIOGRAPHY

1.   Well so talking about myself can't be the way,
                              Manabda
No way that portion of air and water seen with my
                    own eyes
Clay shards can't be the way, nor on the curb
          nutshells unswept since who knows when
No way the old oak, branches hanging over
with bats and heart's desires, in hundreds of wishes, filled
          and unfulfilled, wrapped round pebbles
and hanging over swing, swing and splash
          Into the river can't be the way.
No way the river, on its bank the boats for
                              repair,
hammers banging on upturned hulls.
          It can't be the way.

No way the dot on forehead, off-center and green
smudged eyeliner
Trace of turmeric smudge on nose
and row on row of neat blue-border white sarees
              on the move, no way the 10 AM
bicycle chase, unavailing as ding dong ding dong
                    the bell goes
Or the pickle cart and its 21 belljars.
          It can't be the way.

No way the teacher's cane
and chalk and eraser and quotient and sum, and
being stood up on the bench can't be the way.
Period after period the rubbed off words and
                    numbers and
letters and equations and even after hours

on the great black blackboard, still visible
foggy and half-smudged, whole lifetimes and epochs
and their flora and fauna and firestorms and ice–
                                falls,
And even the sudden great comet can't be
                        the way, big brother.
No more than going through one to two to number
                        three fire-tunnel,
and my automatic motion to its very far end, one
early morning…

2.   The lady I live with, when she gets really mad,
and scratches bites tears me to bits, the bruise
marks can't be the way.
When she beats me with a notebook and
                            throws me out
and cast out abroad in the afternoon I go,
                    from my cave
stone weapon slung on shoulder in search of prey
the going out is no way out.
And when in the afternoon I, Thakurdas, alone and
                            loitering,
in every lane turn up
grain store and grocer and
local teashop infested with goons and run by Big
                        Sis-in-Law
And I discover this owner's widow
who like her husband still sells tea
                        a cup for 80 p
and duly in her book enters the dates, the debtors
                    and also the payers up
and I steal a peep to see if she enters my
                    thrashing-with-scrapbook.
But neither book nor thrashing can be the way, big
                            brother,
although the thrashing loosens pages, and letters
                        from my manuscript
go buzz buzz flying far beyond me,
Go far beyond the many ways of burning,
the way of the solar system,

and there is day and there is night
and there is day and there is night.
And on the afternoon of the strike in front of me
a vast ocean dries up on Calcutta's streets.
An ocean lies silent.
The buildings sink beneath,
no sign of the bridges.
The ocean, devoid of people, dries in bright sunlight.
Sometimes a police jeep shows on the surface,
shakes off the water.
The ocean dries.
There is day and there is night
There is night and there is day
But day and night can't be the way, older brother,
although their meeting begets a song
which turns into a fox with wings.
The song wheels overhead with open jaws
and in the glitter of its wings I see him,
my onetime musical friend,
that was the E! He could see even in darkness
There's the F! I'd see,
but at this moment I see him
on the roof of a skyscraper,
at this moment he sees me
on the roof of that high-rise.
On its edge we grapple and push each other
over a woman.
From which edge we both slip and drop
through cloud and moon
through rain and mist
Twirling we drop and still drop
till down we smash into pieces, one
early morning...

3.   That early morning I wake on a mound,
and the novel begins.
From my right the fire comes out,
          from my left the fire comes out.
Inside a ruined chapel
Sadhan Mondol gets caught with his sister's
                    daughter,

and the noise drives out the fluttering hens,
on the wall the rooster crows,
and the novel begins.
Raising dust the noise fades out, and through
Shatigachha, Ramnagar and Humnipota, day after day,
                    goes on
my wandering.
And suddenly in front of me appears
the weed-overgrown Chaudhuri mansion, and on
                    its crumbled column
the upsprung, neck-twisting chameleon.
For philandery, this house stands lost to weeds
For suicide, for giving up the land,
for secrets, for holy fire and libation,
for secret chambers and vengeance,
for lust and its dark combustion
No lamp burns on the hearth because
                    lighting up needs a spark.
Man woman together make fire.
From the right the fire comes out, from the left
                    the fire comes out,
thrashing to death on hard young breasts the fire
                    still comes out.
Stabbed again and again by the woman on horseback
                    the fire still comes out.
Darkness comes out too.
This is that darkness
that takes me to another novel.
This is that novel
that takes me to a bridge.
This is that bridge
that takes me to a lady.
This is that lady
who tells me, Come, let's get away.
This is that getaway
that takes me to a hell.
This is that hell
where daily I blame her on every pretext,
and she nags me.
This is that nagging

that drives me out to get my paycheck.
This is the paycheck
on which I bust my word-and-rhythm brain.
This brain blows up the instant it hits ground and
                    lights up every letter,
and the letters rise burning and stick in
                            the trees,
and the burning trees fly, pierce my bearings.
These are the bearings
having lost which I come home at day's end.
This is that home
that at night vanishes silent under the soil,
when she hugs me to her bosom and says
"There's no other way for me"
when I hug her to my bosom and say
"There's no other way for me."
She wants to give me all but her body doesn't
                        come awake,
and like a thing half-sunk in ice cut out, I
recoil in pain break off and take breath,
and sleep and
sleep, I
sleep in a motion that turns me to vapor
And upon my hand there an angel.
This is that angel
who teaches me again to call a spade a spade.
This is that spade
with which on my shoulder, once, I burst through
                    the horizon and came
                to this city,
and with friends for year after year,
knocked chunks off the rockface underground.
This is that underground from which just in time
        some have managed to come up and escape,
and turning, have seen that there's no one left
                        behind.
And some in gas and fire,
        water and rockslab,
        darkness and smoke,
have stayed trapped body to body right in this
                        hell.

This is that hell
that I'm able to kill in the end.
This is that end
from which I start myself again, one
early morning…

4.   White and black, violet and blue,
green and nutbrown, all names.
Which of them is mine?
Which name do I go out with in my bag,
which name do I drop from my pocket to the street,
and before getting into office, which is it that
                    I put on in the john?
Which name becomes a pickpocket,
and which the name the pickpocket can't hide
and leaves in the lurch on the street, after which
              others have to carry me home.
Which is the name?

Bent-over, and stood-up,
straight, and laid-down,
knobbed, and hooked. All these sticks.
Which is mine?
Which do I scare off birds with, and which do
        I carry taking the evening breeze,
which do I step down from the carriage with,
and which do I use to hook down the jackfruit and mango
                    that are out of reach?
Which do I whirl in a flash and
stave off danger coming down from above?
Tapping which on the ground does Oedipus depart
                    the city?
Tapping which on the walls do I come to know
where is
hidden from the Income Tax Department
the bejewelled skeleton?
And which do I put to sleep pillowed on my bed
and myself stand all night leaning against the
                    wall?
Until loaded with its happenings – crash –

like a hard slap on the day the newspaper
                    flies in,
even until my lady over my head
pours cold tea to shake off my sleep
and grabbing me by the hair sends me off to the
                    bazaar.
I stand shivering before vegetables, and before
                    fish
How much for aubergines today how much for
gherkins you'll make us give up fish yet I see
From all around the vendors pluck my feathers off
and coming back from the Jodhpur Park bazaar and
coming back from Gariahat bazaar, I
            the Krishna of Nadia
my two bagfuls of shopping burn furiously
The yearly income keeps burning
Eighteen hundred and fifty for two cubbyholes
                    keeps burning
In my mind I pay the landlord seven rupees extra
and the instant it reaches eighteen hundred and
                    fifty seven I
become one with rebel sepoys
tear the cartridge with my teeth and loading the
                    two bags I set on fire
lake bazaar and Jagubazar
small bazaar and Burrabazar
open market and inflated market
Rajabazar and Kassimbazar
Lalbazar and Kalabazar
The Bengal-Bihar-Orissa market all afire
Howls go up at Lalbazar and the blackmarket
Yellow green blue violet and nutbrown all bazaars
Which one is mine?
            Inside my two bags burn
two cubbyhole spaces
in one of which someone cooks rice for my office lunch and
            lamentation for my fate
In the other stretched on the bed lies my stick
Lies stretched and because there's no love any–
                    where
                in place of me

it's the stick that begins to write love poems one
early morning…

5.   Stick-written Poetry

Some island, some peak, some blue, some dot,
            some limit, some number, some hue,
Some poison, some vapour, some cloud, some blood-
            red, some tear, some eye, some breath
Some choking, some weapon, some roots, some torn,
            some plea, some hurt, some cry,
Some grief, some payback, some hook, some bait,
                        some
palate, some behind, some behind, some
con, some
spiracy

*[Through the window everyone tells the stick: what's all this? Get serious,
now. The stick turns to its right as if it had a right side and starts]*

Some instrument, some player, some Ravi, some
      Shankar, some clown, some hacksaw, some wood
Some plank, some pyre, some corpse, some scavenger,
some priest, some penance, some stick
Some clatter, some crack, some lap, some head,
            some writing, some written, some
love

*[Through the window everyone scolds the stick: Now what have you started?
Quick put your mind to it. The stick turns to its left as if it had a left side
and puts its mind to it]*

Let's have no prickly-herbal patriotic builders
no reverend tremors of pure thrill
no divisive minds bestowing grace on sandbars
no thorn thicket calmly brave or fearful

Let's have no daily springtime lessons in guile
no bighearted swindles free of envy
no high stitchcraft, no instant song on demand
From now only the cocked snook, the hint of a
                        catcall

69

[It's talking nonsense, nonsense. Uproar at the window. Put it to sleep, to sleep. Stick, go to sleep. No need to make love any more.]

Where there's sleep, colors change beneath the
                                        sleep
the hunter's black hand and beside it, a fair hand

Where there's water, underwater the mail van's
upturned wheels next to the hyacinth weeds

In the driver's widow and his spinster
sister's eyes, not a teardrop to weep

Where there's a hangout, men variously drunk
the lightning back and forth draftsman

Where there's a bet, its outcome announced
the fruit, the hole in it, the snake, and Parikshit

Where all is shantytown, whorehouse,
mayhem anytime over the winnings

Mothers bring men home
Dry faced infants wander

Explosives stored in a broken house
A couple of day laborers blown to bits
become twisted lumps of flesh

                In there,
in that writing love has no place whatever!

            Make space

Space that's low, water below, rock below, love's low stables
feed below, tumble low, rise but still low, live in low stables
Labor high, shovel high, window high, by the hour
all toted up
The price of sweat, the price of gold, plate and
                    glass, Shiuli Das

All toted up
One hour, this man, three hours on his chest
Three men
One face comes down, goes up, another face
Not a sign
The price of a bed, the married state, morn and
                        night, the kitchen room
All toted up
Living too is low, space that's low, hearts
                stifling close in low stables
Two in one bed, water between, to cross over
There's just no way
Cross the water
The path low, run low, tumble low, pant, at last
dawn's open mountains
                        High stables
The path to sleep-mountain
To take the early morning path
go early morning.

*[Good show! I come into the room and hail the stick. A great comeback,
you'll get kudos. For a few days I lend the stick my head, press it down on its
neck. And it lends me its spine. Then we set out in a book made of air...]*

6.   What is given in that book

A lifetime's coming through clouds is told here.
Is told how the cyclone spins on one point.
The blue hue of air is told in this book. In an
                        inlet
a lone boat, water trapped in its bottom,
                        wriggling
fish trapped in the water, and fish-filching boys
                in loincloth, yes,
the power of theft is told in this book. The
                        condition
before getting caught and after, how to
                rehabilitate and how,
at any age, free motion can be maintained to and
                        fro

between the states of good man and thief, that's
told right here in this book. Besides, the trick
of burying one's head in the earth, and Gopal the
            amulet seller at the Court corner
and the miracle amulets he sells at every
            crossing in front of the Registry Office
are also told. Talisman of Mother Kamaksha.
dispute over property, dispute over wife, a job
you can't get, throatache, heartburn, premature
                        ejaculation, fear
of ghosts as you come home at night, footsteps
            behind you you turn and no one's there,
Your cure for everything is here, plus the magic
                        you make
With this amulet's amazing action, are also given
in this book. Behind Gopal's unending screen of
                        words
his noisy and unfed family's story is also
here. Now you see it, now you don't.
Here's squabbling among themselves. And the art of
The proffered palm. Beyond a note on "Without you
            Sujata I will die"
There's nothing much about love.
There's also a chapter for poets. On reaching
                  a particular page
in it will be seen a long field.
Far below this field, calm, collected, sublime,
                        insane,
glumfaced and always-smiling poets sit and stand
there. The ones unrecognized in their time. Turn
the page and instantly in the field one after
                        another
lids open up and, like officers from inside a
                        submarine,
uniformed poets take up position.
Plantlife and insects from all around do them
homage. And birds too. The poets wave, walk up
receive their laurels but the next page is
                  darkness. There
afterlife is shaking itself awake. Lifetime
                  legends

are cast into outer space. There, then,
everyone is like an infant. Floating weightless,
helpless. No control over limbs, from deepest blue
Spinning away all vanish, at one point, into a
                              gigantic
ball of fire. Some even shoot out through the
                              flames
scattering light like dancers of gold.
Because, yes, this book also tells how to
                    mix with fire.

7.   The story after the book is read

Into the air I dive and so begins my
swim. Not swimming, crawling I go wrapped in a sheet
inside a half-dark city where one can't tell day
from night. Not city, I go under a huge blanket—
                              wrapped
table where, on either side heavy legs and
     important feet knock together. In that light
and shadow I catch sight of a girl. I tell her,
I have to write a love poem right away. Will you
help me? She inclines her neck and says,
Ye-es! I say, Then take one good look
at me. The way you used to look from the window!
She stares with full eyes and her deep black pupils
give off illuminated numbers and letters,
dashes and dots, data upon data, a table of
                              directions.
I lower my eyes to say, Will you put your palms
together? I want to rest my face in them.
                         She says,
But just this morning two full page ads
have come. Her one palm glitters with
                    suiting-shirting, and
along the other palm runs
a Hero Honda. Pleading I say, Okay then at least
stick out your tongue and make a face! She opens
                    her mouth but
can't close it again. From deep in her throat

up over her tongue come down great rolls
of newsprint, her irises turn upward, I
keep moving ahead on the newsprint and
see ornamental pattern after pattern after pattern
                    drawn on the ground, and
there I see Mother Lakshmi too and at once with
                    both hands
I move to undress them both and no one comes
to stop me, a terrific fanfare sounds and
people come running for the show and I leap
over the mountain of paper, to the other side.

On the other side, water to horizon's end. Nothing
                    living or human about.
At water's edge, on a huge rock, a globe on his
                    shoulder
as in the picture, sits Atlas. At first sight of
                    me
he throws the globe from his shoulder into the
                    water. The globe instantly
goes whoosh to the other side and becomes a half
                    sunset.
He stands up and says, It's not what you think.
                    I am
the ocean, not Atlas. Have you ever written
                    anything
about me? I say, I've never had the chance.
–Well, so now write a lyric poem. I
say, But I'm trying to write a love poem now.
–Try if you want to, but remember, without
writing about the ocean no poet can go back from this earth.
Nor will you. This beach is for you.
Go, write.

     Lyric for the Ocean

     It spilt over, hit me with waves,
           foamed foam all over,
    this ocean
     I put my head in and pulled it out, trying to

bite my neck off up to my chest it broke
                                its teeth,
this ocean
I opened my mouth wide and stayed lying on
                        the sand
until roaring it came at a run and all
        of it went straight into my mouth,
this ocean
I lay down flat and kicking about angrily
like a fountain out of my nose and mouth it
                        shot out,
this ocean
After that smoke and ash, hot mud and bones
It kept erupting till it
                        closed up,
this ocean

As soon as I finish writing I look up to see
in front of me
all the water has dried. One vast dry seabed.
In the sky a strange red glow. Scattered at far
                        intervals lie
skeletons of ancient amphibians and reptiles. Sunk
                in sand
rusty men-of-war, broken cannon muzzles. Gray
                        and
black the rocks. Pieces of an airplane
tail. Only, from far away, across the thousands of
                        miles of stretching
seabed, tripping and falling and picking itself
                up, running on towards me,
my life, and chasing it from behind comes a
                        colossal hornet
and running behind it too a skyful of spiraling
                        dustcloud
inside which you can catch glimpses now and again
of a red giant, our future solar star...chased
and running towards me comes my life and
raises its hands, says, Wait, I can't hear a
                        thing, the wind

blows, sand gets in the eyes, as soon as I try to
                    reach it
bursting out of the dry sea crust rises a
                    man-sized
wallclock, stands in my way, and from its dial
one long hand reaches out to nail me to one rusty
early morning…

8.   Epilogue

After this, there's nothing to call death
Nothing to call a call
Nothing to call honey or ocean
Nothing to call faintness when two eyes meet
Nothing to call immersion in any tide
Wherever you may be I'll wait all my life – not
                    even that

Only where I burn leaves,
the countryside
Only where I dig out dead villages from the sand,
the pilgrim place
Where I dry out funeral attire,
the riverbank
Where all day I ring the bell,
the place of work
Where all our mingling is unburnt ashes,
the earth
cradled with much care and pain in
                the palm of the hand
                    All life long, that
                    piece of desert
where
we shall never again meet, die, cast our shadows
Those asleep will not be left beside the sun
There will be no concealment among the clouds
There will be no green journal
There will be no contention with anyone
to run from under one hanging sword to the next
No new kinds of rock, no flood, no black and green

treeline on the coast, with anyone
and no celebration I will attend the rest
                    of my life
I will not go to the Rongali-Bihu
and say to anyone: Today is the day after death
today is the day after light, the day after dust
the day after sorrow
This day on I won't write love,
only, hiding in my head, I'll carry about
        a scrapbook of lightning and thunder.

Translated by Probir Ghosh

TODAY

All my words a child flung into the fire
All my voices, sounds of triumph, weapons of destruction
All my rhythms a sword raised in slaughter
All my poetry an impaled foetus
All my love nothing, nothing at all
The boy watching his mother's rape

And if today inside my home I save my skin
do not obstruct, but talk about what happened
                            whose fault it was
If I don't block the way, if I can't leap in now, today
all my art just genocide from this day.

Translated by Indranee Ghosh

Glossary
by Subir Datta

Ex-husband
Duggā's mother: is the domestic help. It is a common practice in Bengal to identify a woman as the mother of her child.

Don't Wait for Your Lover Any Longer
Māruti: a popular passenger car in India.

If You Ask Me
Shūndillo/Bhardwāj: two 'gotras' among upper class Hindus. 'Gotra' is a term applied to a clan or a lineage – exogamous and patrilineal – whose members trace their descent to a common ancestor, usually a sage of ancient times.

Durlov: one of the lower castes in the Hindu caste system.

Koiborto: a Hindu caste whose main occupations were agriculture and fishing.

Chandāla: the lowest caste in the Hindu caste system. Usually employed as cleaners and pyre-attendants, chandālas were considered untouchables.

Ashes from a Burnt-out Sun
Jagannāth: literally Lord of the world, it is the name given to a particular image of Vishnu, or more accurately, of Krishna. The image of this God has no legs, and only stumps of arms. Together with Jagannāth are seated his brother Balarām and sister Subhadrā, both without limbs. These three images are worshipped in the same form in all the Jagannāth temples, situated mostly in the eastern parts of India. The temple town Puri in the state of Orissa is the chief center of Jagannāth worship.

Moutāt Maheswar
Moutāt Mahéswar: Shiva is the oldest known godhead figure in the world. In one of his forms the meditating Shiva (or Mahādev or Mahéswar) appears intoxicated with *somā.* This is the nectar of the gods and is probably an ancient name for *bhāng,* which is a beverage made of cannabis leaves, almonds, rose water and milk. The expression, *Moutāt Mahéswar* refers to the poet's own meditations in a state of poetic intoxication.

For a Cloudgirl
sunshine clouddoe: a metaphor derived from the story of Māricha's

81

temptation of Sitāby assuming the guise of a golden doe in the Sanskrit epic *Rāmāyan*. It represents in part a longing for illusive and elusive beauty.

golden doe: in *Rāmayan* Rāma, his wife, Sitā, and his half brother Laksman were in exile in Dandaka forest. The demon king Rāvan decided to abduct Sita of whom he had been enamoured. He ordered his magician, Mārich, to disguise himself as a golden doe and appear before Sitā. When Sitā saw the doe she insisted that she must have it. Leaving Sitā alone, Ram and Laksman went to capture the elusive animal when Rāvana descended from the sky and abducted Sita. This was the genesis of the great battle in *Rāmayan*.

Huntsman, Desist
In 1998 the then Hindu nationalist Government of India exploded a nuclear bomb. Neighboring 'Islamic' Pakistan responded by exploding its own bomb soon after. This is the context of the poem.

Huntsman, Desist: This is an allusion to the Sanskrit phrase, "Mā nishād." When Vālmiki, the supposed author of the Sanskrit epic, *Rāmāyan*, was wandering in the woods he once saw a hunter shoot dead with his arrow the male of a pair of mating birds. While the female lamented the death of her partner Vālmiki uttered a two-line curse on the hunter: *Mā nishād pratisthām twamagahma shāswatih samāh / Jat krounchamithunādekambadhih kāmamohitam* ('Hunter! May you never for eternity find success / For you have killed one of the stork couple absorbed in the act of love'). In the Indian tradition this was the beginning of utterances in formal meter, in other words, of poetry.

stupas: Buddhist monuments, generally of a pyramidal or dome-like form and created over sacred relics of the historical Buddha or on spots consecrated as the scenes of his acts.

Nānak: Nānak was born (CE 1469) a Hindu, but employed later by a Muslim, which gave him knowledge of Islam as well. He became a religious teacher, preaching a new faith based upon ideas from both Hinduism and Islam. This new religion, later called Sikhism, believed in one God and the equality of all human beings. Nānak traveled far and wide to spread the new religion, and wrote his own hymns: the most famous is *Jāpji*, which is chanted at dawn each day. He came to be known as Guru Nānak.

Tulsidās: a 16th century poet who translated the Sanskrit epic *Rāmāyan* into Hindi.

Kabir (b. CE 1440): A weaver by calling, Kabir was a mystic and preached the ideal of seeing all of humanity as one. His philosophy and ideal of devotion to God is expressed through metaphor and diction borrowed from both the Hindu *Vedānta* and *Bhakti* streams (intense devotion, expressed by service and by placing oneself at the mercy of God), and Muslim and Sufi ideals.

Shrirāmcharitmānas: this translation of *Rāmāyan* in Hindi by Tulsidās is widely read in north India. Many of its verses have become popular proverbs in this region and many of its phrases have passed into common speech.

Granth Sahib: Guru Granth Sahib is a collection of devotional hymns and poetry considered to be the supreme spiritual authority of the Sikh religion.

Béhulā: legendary folk heroine and one of the main characters of *Manāsamangal* which belongs to a genre of popular Bengali epic poetry written between the 13th and 18th centuries. This poem describes the greatness of the folk deity Manasā, the goddess of snakes.

Lakhinder: in *Manasāmangal* he is the son of Chānd Saodāgar and husband of Béhulā. Chānd Saodāgar, a devotee of Shiva, had boasted that he was cleverer and stronger than Manasā the snake goddess. He built an iron chamber for Lakhindar, believing it to be impregnable. However, on Béhulé and Lakhindar's wedding night, Manasā sent a snake to kill Lakhindar. The snake made itself as fine as a strand of hair and, entering the chamber through a minute hole, bit Lakhindar. Béhulā refused to accept her husband's death. She placed her husband's corpse on a banana raft and set out on a hazardous journey towards the abode of the gods. Despite all the dangers and temptations she encountered, Béhulā steadfastly continued her journey and finally succeeded in reaching her destination. She pleaded for her husband's life and promised Manasā that Chānd Saodāgar would worship her. Moved by Béhulā's love for her husband, Manasā not only restored Lakhindar but also his brothers whom she had killed earlier. Béhulā returned home with her husband and brothers-in-law, and Chānd Saodāgar finally bowed before the might of Manasā.

Zénd Āvéstā: refers to a collection of sacred texts of the Zoroastrian religion. The word 'Zénd' means commentary or translations. The texts of the Āvéstā proper remain sacrosanct and continue to be recited in Āvéstān – which is considered to be a sacred language.

Lachhmanpur: a village in the Indian state of Bihar where a mass killing took place on the 2nd of December 1997.

Namāz: Muslims say five daily prayers. These are called namāz.

Keralā: Keralā is on the southernmost tip of India. It stretches along the coast of the Arabian Sea and is separated from the rest of the subcontinent by the steep Western Ghāts. Keralā is the cradle of Christianity in India. Christianity took root on the Mālābar Coast (now Keralā) in the first century CE around the seven churches that St. Thomas established there. Christian faith has since flourished across the land, coexisting with other religions. Now eleven of the twenty three dioceses in India are in Keralā.

Ajantā's chamber: the first Buddhist cave monuments at Ajantā date from the 2nd and 1st centuries BCE During the Gupta period (5th and 6th centuries CE), many more richly decorated caves were added to the original group. The paintings and sculptures of Ajantā, considered masterpieces of Buddhist religious art, have had a considerable artistic influence.

Padmapāni: the lotus-bearer; the name in Tibetan mysticism of the Bodhisattva Chénrézi, equivalent to the Sanskrit Avalokitesvara.

Awalokiteswar: this is a term commonly employed in Buddhism, and concerning which a number of intricate and complex teachings exist. Technically Avalokitesvara is the dhyani-Bodhisattva of Amitābha-Buddha. Amitābha-Buddha is the cosmic divine monad of which the dhyani-Bodhisattva is the individualized spiritual ray, and of this again, the manushya-Buddha or human Buddha is a ray or offspring.

'Little Buddha': this is a reference to India's first nuclear test, carried out in May 1974, which was code named the 'Smiling Buddha'. The coded message sent by the scientists at the site to the then Prime Minister Indira Gandhi to signify success was "Buddha has smiled."

Parswanāth: According to Jainism, there has been a cycle of 24 Tirthankars. The 23rd Tirthankar Paraswanath was born at Vārānasi in BCE 877. After rigorous penances as an ascetic he attained salvation in BCE 777 at Mt. Paraswanāth in the present Indian state of Bihar.

Tirthankar: In Jainism, a Tirthankar (also Tirthankara or Jinā) is a human who, by adopting asceticism, achieves enlightenment and thus becomes a Jinā (one who has conquered his inner enemies - anger, pride, deceit, desire etc.).

Padmā: the downstream of the river Gangā, more precisely, the combined flow of the Gangā and the Brahmaputra after their confluence at Goālandaghāt in Bangladesh.

Bhātiāli: a popular musical form composed and sung by boatmen in Southern Bangladesh.

Jamuna: a river in northern India which rises in the Himalayas. The rivers Gangā and Jamuna are two of the most sacred rivers in India.

Shyam: dark-complexioned, one of the names of the Lord Krishna.

Rāi: adolescent Rādhā, the beloved of Lord Krishna.

Meerābai: 16th century devotee of Lord Krishna. She was born a princess and was married into a royal family, but gave up everything and endured persecution. Her devotional songs are popular even today.

Mahābhārat: the great Sanskrit epic considered the longest poem in the world.

Essay Concerning Light
Bandé Āli Miā (1906-1979): Bangladeshi poet, novelist, playwright and writer of children's literature.

Shiuli: Latin *Nyctanthes arbor-tristis*, a deciduous tree whose star-shaped flowers with orange stems exude an exotic scent, blooming at night and falling at dawn. The shiuli is a metaphor for beauty and transience.

Gangāsāgar: 130 kilometres from Kolkata, Gangāsāgar is the popular name given to the point where the Gangā merges into the Bay of Bengal. Located on the western edge of the Sunderban delta, it is a part of the Sāgar island. Thousands throng to Gangāsāgar on the occasion of Makar Sankrānti (January 14-15) to bathe in the sea to wash away their sins and to attain salvation. Makar means Capricorn and Sankrānti is transition. There is a sankrānti every month when the sun passes from one sign of the zodiac to the next.

Nagérbāzār: a residential and commercial area in northeast Kolkata.

Part Autobiography
Mānabdā: Mānabéndra Bandyopādhāy. See author's interview for details.

Thākurdās: Ishwar Chandra Vidyāsāgar's father. Vidyāsāgar, known for his contribution to education and social reform, and for his pioneering work in the development of Bengali prose, writing on his father, mentions an incident when one afternoon, driven by hunger and a constant battle against poverty, Thākurdās left his home. That afternoon he came across a shop that sold puffed and pressed rice, run by an elderly widow. Taking pity on him she gave him food to eat although he had no money to pay her. The poet had read about this in a school textbook in his childhood. Among the images and events that rose to the surface of memory in the composition of this long poem, the remembrance of this text is one.

Shātigāchhā, Rāmnagar, Humnipotā: rural regions in Nadiā district, West Bengal.

Rebel sépoys: Indian soldiers of the British Indian Army mutinied in 1857 starting a year-long insurrection against the British. The mutineers then marched to Delhi and offered their services to the Mughal emperor, whose predecessors had been ignobly defeated by the British a hundred years earlier at the battle of Plassey. The insurrection was sparked by the introduction of cartridges rumoured to have been greased with pig and cow fat, which was offensive to the religious beliefs of Muslim and Hindu sépoys (soldiers). In a wider sense, the insurrection was a reaction by the indigenous population to rapid changes in the social order engineered by the British over the preceding century and an abortive attempt by the Muslims to resurrect a dying political order.

Jodhpur Park: a residential area in south Kolkata.

Gariāhāt Bāzār: the big market place in south Kolkata.

Krishna of Nadiā: Sri Chaitanya Mahāprabhu, born in 1496 CE, lived the first half of his life in the district of Nadiā in West Bengal, as a householder. In his youth, he was known to be a great scholar. While still a youngster, he journeyed to Gayā in memory of his late father and there he was initiated into the devotional worship of Rādhā and Krishna. On account of his devotional fervor, he was soon recognized as a united avatar of Rādhā and Krishna, emerging as the leader of all Vaishnavas in the area. Vaishnavism is a religious tradition that originated in Bengal of medieval India. It is counted among the devotional bhakti-traditions of Hinduism that hold Vishnu, or Krishna, as the supreme godhead.

Lake bāzār and Jagubāzār: two market places in south Kolkata.

Būrrābāzār: the wholesale market in Kolkata. 'Būrrā' literally means 'big'.

Rājabāzār: a largely Muslim locality in central Kolkata.

Kāsimbāzār: Kāsimbāzār or Cossimbāzār is a town on the river Bhāgirathi in the Murshidābād district of West Bengal, India. Once it was the great trading centre of Bengal, which declined after the foundation of Kolkata. It was famous for its silks, hosiery, korās and beautiful ivory work.

Bengal-Bihar-Orissa: three east Indian states.

Lālbāzār: Kolkata Police Headquarters.

Ravi Shankar: the legendary sitārist and composer is India's most well known musical Ambassador to the West.

Parikshit: in the Sanskrit epic *Mahābhārat* he is the son of Abhimanyu by his wife Uttarā, and grandson of Arjun. He was killed by Aswatthāman in the womb of his mother and was born dead. But he was brought to life by Krishna, who blessed him and put a curse on Aswatthaman. When Yudhishthira retired from the world, Parikshit succeeded him to the throne of Hastinapurā.

Shiuli Dās: Shiuli is a common female name in Bengali. 'Dās' is a surname.

Mother Kāmākshā: The temple of Kāmākshā is one of the main temples dedicated to the Mother Goddess in India. Mythology and folklore give us many stories about the origin of the temple. It is generally believed that it was built where a part of the dead body of Sati, the wife of Shiva, fell after Vishnu had cut it asunder with his Sudarsana Chakra. This temple contains no image of the Goddess, but in the depths of the shrine is a cleft in the stone, adored as the yoni of Sati. To this day, Kāmākshā remains the symbol of man's aspiration to achieve mastery over the secret laws of the occult world.

Mother Lakshmi: Lakshmi is the Hindu goddess of wealth, fortune, beauty, pleasure, and abundance – all the goods things in life. She is the consort of Vishnu, and is his wife in each of his incarnations. Usually Lakshmi is depicted sitting on a lotus, wearing a red sari, covered in jewels. In one of her four hands she holds a vase containing fortune and wealth.

Rangāli Bihu: Bihu is one of the most important festivals in the north-eastern state of Assam. There are three such festivals in Assam: in the months of *Bohāg* (mid April), *Māgh* (mid January), and *Kāti* (mid October). The Bohāg Bihu (also called as Rangāli Bihu or the Festival of Merriment) marks the beginning of the New Year – the seeding time. The Kāti Bihu (also called Kongāli Bihu or the Festival of the Poor) marks the completion of sowing and transplanting of paddies. The Māgh Bihu (also called Bhogāli Bihu or the Festival of Food) marks the end of the harvesting period. Of all the three, the Bohāg Bihu or the Rangāli Bihu is the period of greatest enjoyment, marking the arrival of spring.

Today
This poem was written during the Gujrāt genocide in 2002 involving fatal attacks on the Muslim minority in the state by mobs of Hindus with the active collaboration of the State machinery. It was reprinted in Shāshokér Proti ('Addressed to the Ruler') – a collection of poems written after the Nandigrām killings on March 14, 2007. In Nandigrām at least 14 villagers, protesting against agricultural land acquisition to build a chemical hub, were killed when police opened fire. The casualty, West Bengal's worst in thirty years of Left rule, sparked off nation-wide protests. For the poet, both Gujrāt of 2002 and Nandigrām of 2007 represent the same kind of state sponsored terrorism.

Sumit Chakrabarti in
Conversation with Joy Goswami

SUMIT CHAKRABARTI: This is the first edition of translations of your poetry. How do you look at translations? Do you think it's possible to capture both the rhythm of a poem and its content in a translation? Is it necessary?

JOY GOSWAMI: I'm satisfied with my Bengali language readership. I really didn't have the aspiration that my works would be read in other languages. There's always the possibility that some parts of a poem will be lost in translation. The subject of my poems has always been more important to me than rhythm or meter. It is enough that the spirit of a poem is captured in the translation. I'm quite satisfied with the translations in this volume.

SC: I have heard about your experiences in Iowa where you worked with Skye Lavin on the translations of your poetry. Skye didn't know much of Bengali. So the two of you sat with dictionaries and fumbled for the right words. How did you go about it?

JG: When we first met, we translated eleven poems in ten weeks. Later when I went to the US in 2003 we met again and translated three more poems. It was a new and wonderful experience for me... we almost journeyed through the poems, both Skye and me. It was also very exciting for Skye. She confessed this not only during those ten weeks, but later on through e-mails as well. It was exciting for her because she was journeying through poems in a language unknown to her. It was thrilling for me because a poet generally doesn't go back to his poems once they have been composed, printed and published. While translating I had to journey through a poem time and again, and I made strange discoveries, and of course found faults as well. And Skye, while traveling through an unknown poem, was discovering myriad things. Now let me tell you the method we used. First, I translated for her the words in a line into English and she would note it on her laptop. Then she would want me to locate the verbs. This took us a long time. Initially we sat on Fridays, but later on we met almost every day. Say, we began at three in the afternoon and continued till ten, ten thirty at night. That's because it generally took three to three and a half hours for the body/words of a poem to reach her. She used to transfer each poem in its raw form on her computer and leave for home. And then we used to speak through the night or from the morning over the phone. She would ask about the nuances and the turns of phrases...and since we lived close by she often drove to my place. The next day being a Saturday we sometimes worked throughout the day. Thus we got a chance to travel through my poems, and a part of this experience is captured in at least two poems in this collection. And I think my readers will like these two poems.

SC: I have noticed a clash between the rigor of meter on the one hand and an explosion of images on the other in your poems from the beginning. When the words occur to you do they come automatically in a metric form, or is the meter imposed later on to rule the words? Which of these aspects is important to you – the discipline of meter or the ecstasy of words?

JG: The answer is in the question itself. Yes, the words occur in a metric form. Two or three lines come in a flash. Or…may be…just one. The first line grows into the next few lines. The meter is there in the first line itself. Some lines occur automatically in a conventional metrical pattern, and hence I don't have to impose a meter on them. However, neither the meter nor the words have been important for me. What is uppermost is the subject. And I must say here that I cannot decide upon a subject beforehand. As the words begin to come in a rush I suddenly realize 'O, so this is what I'm writing about!'

SC: As a reader of your poems I have sometimes felt that you are trying to free yourself from the discipline of meter…that the words are pushing you from behind with a tremendous energy and trying to throw the meter out of the poem…

JG: When the lines come, they come more or less in the form that you finally see them. Sometimes there is a metrical pattern in the lines and sometimes there isn't…it's almost like open prose. Let's say, in the poem 'Part Autobiography' it started to come in the way you find it. I had once read a piece by Manabendra Bandyopadhay somewhere. This incited a sort of a debate in my mind, but there was no way I could go and argue it out with him… suddenly when I began writing this poem the word 'Manabda' started to occur. But it's not that the argument was carried on in the poem, it was only there at the beginning. This was entirely a prose poem. But the word 'Manabda' came from somewhere unknown…what was the line… "Well so talking about myself can't be the way Manabda". See how the poem begins as an answer to Manabda, this was perhaps due to the fact that I was continuing catechism within myself. But the argument was never continued in the poem. The poem moved on groping for its own way, and so did I, groping for my own. Then, I never faltered for a meter, I wrote as the words came to me. It took me seven days to write the poem. But I never felt that I was consciously trying to move out of any metrical pattern.

SC: Yes, but have you ever felt that as the words come in a rush, the meter tries to restrain them deliberately...

JG: No, it never happens that way. When the words start coming, they come with such force, that they automatically form a pattern...that's the form they take, even I have no control over that. It's only that when I look inside I can just about see the form which they finally acquire. And since I do look inside there are... may be...certain corrections.

SC: I have sometimes noticed a similarity between your poems and the poems of Jibanananda Das. I mean, in the way you handle time. For example, in *Pratnajeeb* ('Primeval Creature') or in *Āléyā hrad* ('Mirage Lake') it seems as if you drag the contemporary with you and move inside memory. You go back into the past with a tremendous velocity, into some kind of an impersonal time where the past and the present become one. Am I right?

JG: From the very beginning I had this tendency of mixing up the past and the present, or let's say all the three time frames of the past, the present and the future. But in some phases they are obvious and in some phases they are a bit implicit. That's it.

SC: To continue in the same vein let me ask you about the way in which love, sexuality, death, rebirth, sudden transcendence have come within this play with time. And within this game there's always the presence of a I/me/myself. Who is this I? The poet himself? Is this journey into impersonal time through a kind of subjectivity where you coalesce your poetic self with a dialogic, universal, timeless poetic self? I particularly have in mind the poems like *Pāgli tomār sangé* ('With You, Mad Woman'), *Ālo Samparkita Probondho* ('Essay Concerning Light'), *Āj jadi āmāké jiggésh karo* ('If You Ask Me Today').

JG: Many poems in *Pratnajeeb* as well...

SC: Yes, many poems in *Pratnajeeb* as well.

JG: Yes, you are absolutely correct. Actually, love, sexuality, death are sometimes literally personal...sometimes somebody else's life has walked over my poems wearing my garments...no, not wearing my garments, but almost as my own self. Sometimes my own life is transferred vicariously into somebody else in some of my poems. For example, *Mālatibālā Bālikā Bidyālaya* ('Malatibala Girls' School')…

SC: Let me interrupt…the French theorist Roland Barthes has spoken about the death of the author. The author relinquishes all right to his text as soon as he completes it. The reader interprets it in his own way. You have called your book *Part Autobiography*…can the poems in this book really be read in the same manner?

JG: I'll say two things here. This will be a longish answer. I had once written the lines "*Āgun tumi kaemon korey hājir koro aemon shob pagol meyeder/ Āmi notun korey chomkey uthi, notun korey ābār bhoi pai*" ('Fire, how do you bring before me such mad girls as these/ I startle anew, I fear afresh'). A few days after this poem was published a student from Guwahati University wrote to me, "How did you come to know about the girls in my university?" Thus he is viewing the poem completely independent of my life, with reference to his own. He's reading this poem in terms of the girls he has known, and it's obvious that I had written the poem with a different girl in mind. I had a friend Chandan, who is no more, who was betrothed for quite sometime, and everybody knew that he was committed to somebody. But one of this girl's friends used to like him a lot. On a *Shivarātri* day this girl gave him a Cadbury chocolate in my presence. And Chandan said to me, "See! What do I do with this mad girl!" And I wrote this poem. So you see, how this poem comes out of an experience which is not directly associated with my own life. Now, somebody from Guwahati University, whom I don't know till date, linked these lines with his own life. This is the first part of my answer.

Now let me talk about what constitutes my autobiography. Say for example, within the course of my life things are happening in Nandigram[1], in the World Trade Center. All of these are part of my autobiography. And then if I fall in love with a girl, that's also part of my autobiography. I suffer from a serious ailment and recuperate in the hospital, that's also part of my autobiography. In 1987 the scientists came to know about the Supernova, that when it exploded the world was not yet born. After such a long time a flash of light from that explosion has reached the earth.

---

[1] In Nandigram, West Bengal, at least 14 villagers, protesting against agricultural land acquisition to build a chemical hub, were killed when police opened fire on March 14, 2007. The casualty, West Bengal's worst in 30 years of Left Front rule, sparked off nation-wide protests.

As soon as I came to know of this in 1987 I started ageing backwards. In a moment this entire time, even before the earth was born, became a part of my autobiography. Thus I have named my poem and my book *Part Autobiography*. Even when I have read somebody else's poems, I have related that to my own life. This is how I learned to read poetry, or how the poems hit me, or came to me. Let's think about life as a sugar solution. The lines of poetry descend this solution as thin threads, and my familiar experiences are crystallized in it, and thus some kind of meaning emerges. For me, these crystals are the meanings of my poems. These meanings can vary from person to person, I have no issues with that.

SC: Bauls and Fakirs are present frequently in your poems. They also become a part of nature…in a way. At the same time, they also have a well defined public role, a certain social responsibility, a mass appeal. Did this ever attract you?

JG: The words in the songs that they sing are almost entirely symbolic. They talk about a secret form of worship through these songs. This is like poetry, because poetry also hides something as it reveals something. The language of poetry is also symbolic. If you want to know the meaning of a Baul's song, you have to mingle with him, live his life, or else he'll not part with his meaning. The philosophy of their worship is what they reveal and hide at the same time in their songs. Here is the connection between the Baul and the modern poet. Another thing…why are the Bauls so secretive about the philosophy of their worship? Because the upper caste Hindus and Muslims categorically oppressed these Bauls, irrespective of their religion. So, these Bauls divided themselves into small groups and created symbolic tunnels through their songs to reach out to one another. Likewise, if you think of our contemporary poets -- except may be one or two privileged ones who kowtow to the centers of power – they are also a minority, divided into small groups. For example, see Kolkata itself, there are so many small groups of poets. This is where I have found a similarity between the Bauls and the poets. Initially we start talking about ourselves, but in the last analysis, perhaps, it embraces everybody. We cannot stop this…

SC: …but then, the Bauls talk to the common people, but the modern poet is often obscure. The Baul has a mass appeal, whereas the modern poet cannot always reach out to the masses. Isn't it so? Do you try to reconcile these two facets?

JG: I would say…

SC: …I mean, do you talk to the common people in your poetry?

JG: I feel my poetry sometimes talks to the common people. At other times it ruminates alone inside closed doors…my poems that is…for example, *Surjyo Pora Chhai* ('Ashes from a Burnt out Sun'), or *Moutat Maheswar, or Aek* ('One'). At other times it talks to the common people! I can say something about why poetry is sometimes obscure. Didn't you just ask why poetry is obscure…

SC: Yes…some of your poems are really obscure. It requires a lot of labor to read them…

JG: Right…when a poem comes to me, I have already told you, how it comes out of my own life, the twenty-four hours that I live everyday. When I write about the Supernova…of a time before creation…I come to know about it within the span of the twenty-four hours of my life. Maybe from a film, or a book, or may be newspaper. That is to say, I experience all of these within this lived experience of twenty-four hours. Some of these experiences are quite rational. For example, the fact that I'm talking to you now…or when I take a sip from this cup of tea. I'm answering into this recorder as and when you are asking me to…and you are pressing the pause button when I'm taking a call on my cell phone. All of these are rationally laid out. I went to my office in the morning, came back home, now I'm here, my daughter called just now to tell me that she was coming here – all of these are rational. Now I'll go home and go off to sleep. But in my sleep, within that span of three or four or five hours, I'll dream…I dream every night. I'll see absurd things in my dreams, every day these dreams come back to me. Sometimes they are so real that I sit up on my bed, dumbfounded. Even today I was awoken by a dream at four thirty in the morning. These events that I perceive in my dreams are absurd, but when I see them within a dream they do not appear so, they seem to be very real. I cannot explain why I see these dreams…if I remember them that is…in fragments. Thus, within this span of twenty-four hours I continuously confront a part of my life that I cannot rationally explain. And my poetry is created out of this twenty-four hours of my life, the lived experience, both rational and irrational. The irrational is ever present, the hazy, the unreal, the unknown…experiences that I pass through every day. This is my world of dreams. It's unknown to me. I also write about these, but you'll notice that only a small portion of my body of poems contain these, as the least portion of my twenty four hours is spent in dreams. I feel fortunate that I have been able to write about these experiences as well, this, my world of dreams, in my poetry. I cannot expect my readers to understand what I don't understand myself. But I go through these experiences, and so I write about them. One thing I must say, that there's a strange romance in being able to put into words the unprecedented juxtaposition of the extraordinary and the surreal.

SC: We have digressed a bit...we were talking about the Bauls and Fakirs and their public role. Let's talk about your most recent book of poems *Shashoker Proti* ('To the Ruler'). You seem to be very angry here and there's also a reflection of the anger of the masses in these poems. It seems as if this constitutes your duty as an intellectual. Edward Said had once said that the chief function of the intellectual is 'speaking truth to power.' Are you doing the same here?

JG: I have written poems like these earlier. In *Santān Santoti* for example... the incidents of Dhantala[2], or the Iraq war, or during the Gujrat massacre[3]. That's because I'm also a part of this society, as everybody else is. I go through life like any other commoner, and every moment I feel the burden of living. When there's a mass homicide I also feel the way you feel. This is an expression of a personal grievance which has coalesced with the grievance of the common people. It's not as if I've written these poems as an intellectual...nothing of that sort. I would have written poems of despair if I were sick. Likewise, this despair is on seeing a malady within society...this angry outburst.

SC: Yes, but you have appeared on television, you have gone to meetings, decrying these incidents. This is perhaps the first time you have done such a thing...

JG: True. I never thought that I would have to speak in public meetings or press conferences against the government. But what happened in

---

[2] On February 5, 2003 women members of a marriage party were raped and murdered by dacoits in Dhantala, Nadia in West Bengal.

[3] Refers to incidents that took place in the state of Gujarat in the year 2002 involving fatal attacks on the Muslim minority in the state by mobs of the majority community.

Nandigram, the heinous crime that was committed made me decide that I would speak up on this issue. It was a call from within...and so I did it. Earlier I used to write prose, I have written about the incidents at Dhantala. After Nandigram I felt that I had to write something, so I wrote these poems. The people wanted me to say something and I also wanted to write something...so these poems happened.

SC: Don't you fear, sometimes, that your pen will stop? That one day you might not be able to write any more?

JG: Yes. This is a very real fear. But then my entire life has been a failure. I failed my mother as a son, my brother as a sibling, my teachers as a student, my friends as a friend, my wife as a husband, my daughter as a father. They have told me this and I know it. If my pen stops I have to carry that burden on my shoulders alone. But if it stops...it stops, what can I do?

SC: You were talking about your dreams. Don't you dream of this failure?

JG: Why should I dream about this? It happens in reality. Once I had not written for a stretch of eleven months or almost a year.

SC: One last question. In a private conversation with me, just after the death of Binoy Majumdar, you had said that a poet is not safe even after his death. Why had you said this?

JG: I could write an essay on this topic. It can't be discussed within such a short space of an interview. In our country, a poet is evaluated either during his lifetime, or immediately after his death. Those who do this are almost contemporaries of this poet. They generally discuss his personal life or idiosyncrasies or some behavioral traits, and these become more important in the discussion of his poems. This is true for novelists or film makers as well. These personal details are perhaps irrelevant in terms of the appreciation or evaluation of his poetry. Ideally we should talk about what he wrote, his poems – what they give us. How can someone judge a poet by his external behavior, when writing a poem is a very internal process? He still has a chance to explain himself during his life time, but he is so helpless after his death. People can say anything about him. I think both Binoy Majumdar and Shakti Chattopadhay have been evaluated in this manner. Anecdotes about Shakti's drunkenness or Binoy's eccentricities have only hindered a true appreciation of their poems. They were helpless after their death. I think they can be properly evaluated only by a generation that comes fifty years later, who were not even born when these poets were writing. They can evaluate the poets objectively, free from the external influences of those who knew the poets personally, who spread such personal and irrelevant stories about them.

SC: Don't you fear your own death?

JG: Yes, I do. It's a major fear.

Poems of Joy Goswami,
Bengali Editions

Kabita Songroho (in 3 Vols), (Collected Poems)
Ananda Publishers; Kolkata
Vol. 1, 1990; ISBN:81-7066-205-2; 6th reprint 2001
Vol. 2, 1997; ISBN:81-7215-750-9; 3rd reprint 2002
Vol. 3, 2000; ISBN:81-7756-088-3; 2000

Chrismas o Sheeter Sonetguchchha, 1977
Reprinted by Pratibhash, Kolkata, 2007

Pratnajeeb, 1978
Reprinted by Pratibhash, Kolkata, 2007

Aleya Hrad, 1981
Reprinted by Pratibhash, Kolkata, 2007

Unmaader Pathakram, 1986
Shubachan, Kolkata

Bhutum Bhagaban, 1988
Reprinted by Pratibhash, Kolkata, 2007

Ghumiyechho Jhaupata, 1989
(Ananda Puraskar, 1990)
Ananda Publishers, Kolkata

Ek, 1990
Reprinted by Pratibhash, Kolkata, 2007

Aj Jodi Amake Jiggesh Karo, 1991
Ananda Publishers, Kolkata
ISBN:81-7066-941-3;

Golla, 1991
Prama Prakashani
Reprinted by Pratibhash, Kolkata, 2007

Paagli Tomar Shonge, 1994
Ananda Publishers, Kolkata
ISBN:81-7215-290-6; 1994
Sahitya Akademi Award, 2000
Reprinted by Ananda Publishers, Kolkata, 2000

Bajrabidyut-bharti Khata,
Ananda Publishers, Kolkata
ISBN:81-7215-399-6; 1995

Pakhi, Hushh, 1995
Kabita Pakkhik, Kolkata

Ohh Swapna !, 1996
Ananda Publishers, Kolkata
ISBN:81-7215-512-3

Pataar Poshak, 1997
Ananda Publishers, Kolkata
ISBN:81-7215-672-3

Bishaad, 1998
Ananda Publishers, Kolkata
ISBN:81-7215-786-X

*Ma Nishad,*1999
Ananda Publishers, Kolkata
ISBN:81-7215-946-3

Tomake, Ashcharjyamoyee, 1999
Bijalpa
Reprinted by Pratibhash, Kolkata, 2007

Surjo-Pora Chhai, 1999
Ananda Publishers, Kolkata
ISBN:81-7215-773-8

Jagotbari, 2000
Ananda Publishers, Kolkata
ISBN:81-7756-107-3

Horiner Jonno Ekok, 2002
Ananda Publishers, Kolkata
ISBN:81-7756-240-1

Premer Kabita, 2003
Ananda Publishers, Kolkata

ISBN:81-7756-341-6

Santan Santati, 2004
Ananda Publishers, Kolkata
ISBN:81-7756-401-3

Bikelbelar Kabita o Ghashphuler Kabi, 2004
Ananda Publishers, Kolkata
ISBN:81-7756-405-6

Moutat Maheswar, 2005
Ananda Publishers, Kolkata
ISBN:81-7756-426-9

Shandhyapheri o Onnanno Kabita, 2006
Ananda Publishers, Kolkata
ISBN:81-7756-561-3

Amar Shyamasri Eechchhay Amar Swagata Eechchhayguli, 2007
Ananda Publishers; Kolkata
ISBN:81-7756-637-7

Shashaker Prati, Bijalpa, 2007

Sherstha Kabita (collection of selected poems), 2008
Pratibhash, Kolkata,

Jara Brishtite Bhijechhilo (Novel in verse), 1998
Ananda Publishers; Kolkata
(Ananda Puraskar, 1998)
ISBN:81-7215-566-2;

Jekhane Bichchhed, (Novel in verse) 2007
Reprinted by Pratibhash, Kolkata,

Hoolora Tuler Pashe, (Rhymes for Children), 2006
Doel, Kolkata
ISBN:81-88943-32-0;

Translators' Biographies

HASSANAL ABDULLAH is the author of 24 books, including 13 collections of poetry. He introduced a new form of sonnets in Bengali, seven-seven stanza and the rhyming scheme: abcdabc efgdefg, and wrote a 304-page epic on searching for the relation between human beings and various aspects of the Universe. Hassanal has translated more than 30 Bengali poets into English and number of poets including Charles Baudelaire, Pablo Neruda, Stanley Kunitz, Nicanor Parra, Thomas Tranströmer, and Wisława Szymborska into Bengali. He is the editor of *Shabdaguchha*, a bilingual poetry journal. Mr. Abdullah, the 2007 finalist for the Queens Borough Poet Laureate, is a NYC High School math teacher.

STANLEY H. BARKAN is the editor/publisher of the Cross-Cultural Review Series of Poetry & Art, which has, to date, published some 400 titles in 55 different languages. His co-translations of Bengali, Hebrew, Italian, Macedonian, Romanian, Russian, Serbian, and Spanish have appeared in many publications, the latest in *Chlenskiy* (New York/Moscow), *The Seventh Quarry* (Wales), and *Shabdaguchha* (New York/Dhaka). His own poetry has been translated into 25 different languages.

CHITRALEKHA BASU'S first book, *Sketches by Hootum the Owl: a Satirist's View of Colonial Calcutta* – a reimagining of the first work of modern Bengali prose written in 1861/62 by Kaliprasanna Sinha – was published in September 2012 by Stree-Samya Books, Calcutta, with a foreword by Amit Chaudhuri. Chitralekha was a journalist for 20 years, having worked in India, the UK, Thailand and China. She is now on a sabbatical to work on her next book and occasionally contributes to *The Times Literary Supplement* (UK) and *The Age/Sydney Morning Herald* (Australia).

CAROLYN B. BROWN was translation coordinator and editor for the International Writing Program at University of Iowa during the 1990s; recently retired from Stanford University Press, she now lives in British Columbia. Her translations of Bengali poetry have appeared most recently in *Language for a New Century: Contemporary Poetry from the Middle East, Asia, and Beyond* (Norton), *Mid-American Review, Modern Poetry in Translation, The Oxford India Anthology of Bengali Literature, Parabaas,* and *Zoland Poetry* (Steerforth Press). A selection of poems by Amiya Chakravarty, titled *Another Shore*, cotranslated with Sarat Kumar Mukhopadhyay, was published in India 2002 by the Sahitya Akademi.

SUMIT CHAKRABARTI teaches at the Department of English, Presidency University, Kolkata, India. His research interests include Postcolonial Theory, Culture Studies, and Nineteenth Century Bengal. He reviews books regularly for a leading vernacular magazine.

SUBIR DATTA has just retired from the Department of English, Rabindra Bharati University, Kolkata after more than thirty years of service.

INDRANEE GHOSH had been teaching English literature and literature in English for the West Bengal Education Service, until her recent retirement. She has two books in press. One is her translation of the memoirs of Kanan Devi, who was one of the earliest film stars in Bengal, which is being published by Zubaan Books. The other is a collection of oral folk myths from the Darjeelng Hills, which she has edited, by Pradhan Press, in Darjeeling.

PROBIR GHOSH is a Calcutta-based writer for hire, on advertising copy for print and Internet, business-related articles, industrial video scripts, movie subtitles, and management gobbledegook. He promises never to try translating poems again.

PRASENJIT GUPTA'S work includes *A Brown Man and Other Stories* and the children's novel *To the Blue King's Castle: Adventures in the Underground Forest as well as Indian Errant*, a critically acclaimed collection of translations from Hindi of Nirmal Verma's short fiction. His translations from Bengali of Ashapurna Debi's stories are collected in *Brahma's Weapon*. Prasenjit, a graduate of the Iowa Writer's Workshop and past recipient of a Fulbright fellowship and a grant from the National Endowment for the Arts, serves with the U.S. Department of State as a diplomat currently posted in Hong Kong.

ROALD HOFFMANN is a chemist and writer at Cornell University in Ithaca, NY. Aside from science, he writes nonfiction, plays, and poetry – six books of his verse have been published, the latest being "Soliton" (2002).

SKYE LAVIN was an Iowa Arts Fellow at the Iowa Writers' Workshop from 2000-2002. She is a public librarian in Cambridge, Mass. and she is working on her first novel.

OINDRILA MUKHERJEE is an Assistant Professor of Writing at Grand Valley State University. She has a PhD in Literature and Creative Writing from the University of Houston. She is a former Creative Writing Fellow in Fiction at Emory University. Oindrila is the fiction editor of Kitaab, a journal of South Asian writing. She writes fiction and non fiction. Her work has most recently appeared or is forthcoming in The Greensboro Review, Salon, The Oxford Anthology of Bengali Literature, Vandal, Indian Voices, Wake, and elsewhere.

Previous Appearances of
Translations

CHITRALEKHA BASU: The translations in this book first appeared in *The Statesman* Sunday features pages in 2001, but have since been revised.

CAROLYN BROWN: Earlier versions of "Victorious" and "Schoolgirl on the Verge of Vanishing" were in published in *Signposts: Bengali Poetry since Independence* (New Delhi: Rupa, 2002).

PRASENJIT GUPTA: "Things Recalled at Night" first appeared in *Parabaas,* www.parabaas.com.

SKYE LAVIN: All the three poems in this book were published in slightly different versions in Parabaas, www.parabaas.com.

OINDRILA MUKHERJEE: Both translations were previously published online in *Parabaas.*

The poems in this book have appeared in different versions in "Part Autobiography: Selected Poems," by Joy Goswami, Worldview Publications, Delhi and Kolkata, 2007

Acknowledgements

I am grateful first of all to Joy Goswami, for entrusting this American edition of a translated selection of poems into my hands. It is a privilege, and a joy. The selection you see here, and the translated versions chosen (there are several available in some instances) were made by Joy Goswami.

It was a mutual friend, the great theoretical chemist Debashis Mukherjee, who first introduced us. And who continues to work on my Bengali education. Debashis put into my head the idea of bringing Joy's poetry to the American reader, and Arup SenGupta put the plan into motion by providing the selection here. Arup's enthusiasm for Joy's poetry kept this project alive.

Abhijit Chakrabarti was wonderful in helping me maintain contact with Joy, and for providing materials and support.

Samir Bhattacharya was extremely helpful to me in helping me compile a list of English translations of Joy's poems, and in putting me in touch with the poets. His work on *Parabaas* is of tremendous value to the world and Bengali communities.

I am not a Bengali speaker or reader. At Cornell, I am immensely grateful to Debashree Ghosh and to Debamita Paul. They sat many hours with me, comparing the translations with the Bengali original, parsing meaning. Without their help, I could not have made sense of some of the poems, nor have been able to make suggestions to the able translators.

With her expert Bengali, Carolyn Brown, one of the translators featured in this book, gave me some valued suggestions in the process; I am most grateful to her. I only wish I had been strong enough to follow some of her advice.

Roald Hoffmann

All poems selected by Roald Hoffmann
Introductory essay "Reflections on the Poems of Joy Goswami" by Roald Hoffmann

First published in softcover in the United States of America by Whale & Star Press, Miami, Florida, info@whaleandstar.com, www.whaleandstar.com

Design Concept: The people of Whale & Star
Lead Publication Coordinator: Angel Hernandez
Copy: Tessa Blumenberg

Cover: Enrique Martínez Celaya, *Crying Boy with Elephant*, 2013

Distributted exclusively by University of Nebraska Press
1111 Lincoln Mall
Lincoln, Nebraska 68588-0630
www.nebraskapress.unl.edu
Tel: 800/755 1105
Fax: 800/526 2617

ISBN: 978-0-9799752-7-1